CROSS RHODES

GOLDUST, OUT OF THE DARKNESS

Dustin Rhodes

GALLERY BOOKS

New York London Toronto Sydney

R

H

CROSS

D

E

S

World
Wrestling
Entertainment®
BOOKS

Gallery Books
A Division of Simon & Schuster, Inc.
1230 Avenue of the Americas
New York, NY 10020

Photos on pages 6, 8, 12, and 13 courtesy of *Pro Wrestling Illustrated*.
Photos on pages 210, 222, and 224 courtesy of Dustin Rhodes.
All other photos © World Wrestling Entertainment, Inc. All Rights Reserved.

First Gallery Books trade paperback edition December 2010

GALLERY BOOKS and colophon are trademarks of Simon & Schuster, Inc.

For information about special discounts for bulk purchases, please contact
Simon & Schuster Special Sales at 1-866-506-1949 or business@simonandschuster.com.

The Simon & Schuster Speakers Bureau can bring authors to your live event.
For more information or to book an event, contact the Simon & Schuster Speakers
Bureau at 1-866-248-3049 or visit our website at www.simonspeakers.com.

Designed by Akasha Archer
Illustration from istockphoto.com

Manufactured in the United States of America

10   9   8   7   6   5   4   3   2   1

Library of Congress Cataloging-in-Publication Data

Rhodes, Dustin.
    Cross Rhodes / by Dustin Rhodes
        p.   cm.
        1. Wrestlers—United States—Biography. 2. Rhodes family. I. Title.
    GV1196.A1R47   2010
    796.8120922—dc22
        [B]   2010022987

ISBN 978-1-4391-9516-1
ISBN 978-1-4391-9517-8 (ebook)

DEDICATION

I dedicate this book to all the people in this world who are having trouble with drugs and alcohol, broken homes and broken families, mothers, daughters, sons, and dads confused about life in general. I dedicate this to my sobriety and the new life I look out at every day clean and sober.

To my family, especially my sister Kristin, once I was lost and now I am found. To my sisters Mandy and Teil, I love you very much. It's the least I can do to keep myself clean and sober for each and every one of you who have done so much for me. I owe it to all of you to be a better person and a better human being, and to leave something good in this world before I die.

To my father and mother, who have always been there for me, I love you very much. Despite all the trials and tribulations we have been through, you have been very good parents. You have taught me valuable lessons in life and I'm happy that we are so strongly connected with one another. It means the world to me. To other mothers and fathers out there who don't have that kind of relationship with your children, find it. Fix your broken relationships somehow, some way. Do whatever it takes to get your family back.

To the angels in my life, my daughter, Dakota, and Ta-rel, the love of my life who has stood by me through thick and thin. Every day for the rest of my life I will treat you with respect, honor, and love. Dakota, I will never love anyone the way I love you. You are the angel who looks over me when I am on the road. When I say my prayers every morning and night, I am thinking about you. You are with me every moment of every day. You opened my eyes to how beautiful life can be when you took my hand and said, "It's going to be okay, Dad." I love you, angel.

contents

PROLOGUE

DYING TO GET INTO
THE MAIN EVENT

I started writing this book years ago while sitting in my pickup truck with a handful of pain pills circulating through my body and a bottle of vodka on the passenger seat. For a little while, the pain turned into more of a dull ache than the full-on attack that I woke up to every morning. With a black pen and blue-lined paper torn from a small note-book, those sessions might as well have been a therapist's couch. I was looking for the truth about me, drug addiction, and the old-school world of sports entertainment that grabbed me as a small child and has never let go.

The first words I wrote are scattered across the top of the first page:

Dying to Get into the Main Event.

In one way or another, I probably was dying. I certainly wasn't living, at least not a life the average person would recognize. Hell, I barely recognized what was happening at the time. Looking back, it was just another example of my art imitating my life.

But that was then, when I couldn't see through a daily haze caused by an addiction to prescription pain medication and the limits of self-medicating's ability to dull the pain, no matter how high the pile of pill and vodka bottles. Yet through it all, one aspect of my life never changed and in some ways has never been stronger than it is today. My love and passion for the business of professional wrestling never wavered, not even in the depths of addiction.

ONE

THE FEVER

My dad, The American Dream, Dusty Rhodes.

I got the fever as a young boy growing up in the long shadows of a big man in Austin, Texas.

The American Dream, Dusty Rhodes, is my dad. As a young boy, all I knew was that my dad was gone all the time. For the most part, my mother, my sister Kristin, and I were left to fend for ourselves. I can remember being five or six years old and seeing my dad come home after a long trip. I was like any other small boy. I wanted to crawl all over my dad when he finally walked through the front door. But he was too tired and his body too sore.

Back then, wrestlers worked territories, and they were gone for months at a time. He might spend two or three weeks in one place, come home, then head off to Japan for a month or more. He would take us places and we would get time with him, but it was always cut short by his schedule. My dad was naturally charismatic and very smart. I certainly didn't understand how smart he was about his career then, but as a little boy all I wanted was more time with him. He was larger than life to me.

On top of the world.

Then, one day, he was gone for good. My parents divorced right around the time I entered first grade at a private Christian school in Austin. I didn't get the chance to know him the way a young boy wants to know his father. I was seven years old when my parents divorced. I remember crying for hours at a time during the days, weeks, and months that followed his departure. Even though he was gone a lot before the divorce, I always knew he'd come walking into the house in his cowboy boots and hat. Divorce meant the exact opposite. My father was gone and he wasn't ever coming back. In those days, his life was rolling along at one hundred miles an hour, and being home with family was the slowest part of his existence.

As his stature grew in the business, the shadow became larger and more difficult for me. I don't know if I have ever wanted anything as much as I wanted to leave Austin and go live with my dad. My mother married three times over the next eight years. Like everyone else, she made some bad decisions. The first two stepfathers beat the hell out of my mother. Kristin and I would crouch in the hallway just off the living room. I wasn't old enough to do anything to them physically. We'd just sit there with our backs against the wall listening to the violence. No child should have to live through that. We watched one man after another come into her life, and each one of them did the same thing.

My mother protected herself as best she could.

Incredibly, she took care of us and made sure we never en-
dured what she did. In every other way, my mom took care
of us and never complained. She worked as many as three
jobs and held together what little we had. She was a great
mom, but sometimes stuff happens. Everybody makes bad
decisions here and there. That's life. My mom was a hair-
dresser and she'd put in as many hours as possible, sometimes working at two different salons. When she wasn't
doing hair, my mom cleaned houses and did whatever it
took to make ends meet.

I'm sure all those men beating up my mother contrib-
uted to my desire to leave, but all I remember is crying
a lot. It was just one incident after another. I don't know
how we became so dysfunctional that we allowed bad
people into our lives. Maybe we attracted them in some
way we didn't realize. Maybe my mother had so much
guilt about one thing or another that she felt like she
didn't deserve anything better. I remember one time, my
mom and second stepdad came home, and both of them
were getting out of the truck fighting. Jack and my mother
were screaming and yelling at each other. She swung at
him and he was shoving my mother into the cab of the
truck. She got out and took a swing at him and he grabbed
her hand and yanked it backward and broke her finger.
Her wedding ring flew off her finger out into the grass
near the front of the house. She came inside the house

crying. Her finger was bent to one side. It's hard for a child to process that kind of scene. But as soon as he left I went outside. I must have spent four or five hours combing through the grass looking for that ring. Finally around nine or ten o'clock at night, I found the ring. I walked back inside and gave it to her. I was probably eight or nine years old, and the only comfort I could provide my mother was to find that ring.

Looking back, it seems strange that I was trying to find a symbol of a busted marriage that had just led to a broken finger. I didn't know what else to do or how else to help. I don't know whether my father knew what was happening to my mother. I don't know whether he cared one way or another at the time. My father never failed to send us child support, but he was young and I really don't know whether he gave a damn. Like I said, his life was rolling and on the upswing. He was hell-bent on making a name in the business, which he most certainly did.

After they divorced, my dad would roll into town from time to time and we would go to the events. Still, it wasn't until I was eleven or twelve that I really understood he was famous, or that he did something different from all the other dads. That's about the time I started watching the World Class Championship Wrestling out of Texas with the Von Erichs. Kerry Von Erich, the Modern Day Warrior, was big at that time. The Freebirds were big, too. I remember going to the Coliseum in downtown Austin to see my dad wrestle. I was probably about nine years old, and it was the first time I saw my dad perform live. I was running around the floor as the show was going on. I was so excited to see my dad, and there were all these people jumping up and down cheering for him. It was really cool seeing people react to my dad that way. It was the way I felt about him, too.

Dad versus Ric Flair.

After the show ended, I walked up to the ring. I jumped up onto the apron and grabbed the ropes. That's when I heard my dad's booming voice. He was in the back

I learned from the best.

behind the curtain. He came running out into the arena and started yelling. "Don't you ever get into that wrestling ring again." He was mad, and it was scary for a young boy. I mean, that was my dad. He scared me so much that I didn't get back into a ring until I got my start a decade later. To this day I don't know whether he was concerned about my safety, or he just didn't want me ever to become comfortable with the idea of one day being in the business. I know one thing: I've never forgotten that experience. All I wanted was to be with my dad. It was as if all these people, all the fans in that arena and in cities all over the territories he worked, had more of him than I did. He was always good to us, but I wanted to be a larger part of his life. Many years later my daughter, Dakota, would come with her mother and me on the road. I always let her climb into the ring and bounce around with Hunter and Edge and just have fun.

As the years rolled on, my sister and I didn't see a whole lot of our father. During Christmas, he would fly us to Tampa on Braniff Airlines. In the summer, we'd make the same trip again, this time staying for a month. That's all we really saw of him. Even then he was gone working all the time. Once in a while we talked to him on the phone, but otherwise he was somewhere out in the world. When we did see him, the time passed so quickly that it seemed like within moments of our arrival it was time to turn around and go home. At Christmas we'd open our presents and, *boom*, a couple days would pass and we were headed back to the airport. He was never really there for us. Then again, this lifestyle comes with the territory. It's more demanding than most people can imagine. He was a father when it came to child support and generally doing the right thing in terms of his responsibilities to us, but it was more of a formality. His life was so much bigger, and there wasn't a whole lot of room left for us.

I don't know why my dad chose his path, but he knew how to make just about everyone love him. It is awesome to see. As soon as I became conscious of it, I wanted to be a part of it all. I didn't recognize the fact that sometimes the life is far from glamorous, or that the travel and physical toll can wear you down. Dusty Rhodes was my dad, and I was drawn to him in the same way a fan is. Meanwhile, his career just kept rising. It was like he could do no wrong, and all I saw was the wonder of it all. Everything was going for him and I wanted a life just like his. I wanted that experience. In some ways we were growing up together, though we remained far apart. It seemed like the older I got the bigger he became.

After my sophomore year at Lanier High School in Austin, my mother finally agreed to let me go live with my father. I'm sure she thought, "Okay, go find out for yourself what it's really all about." I was a tight end on my high school football team and I had a lot of friends, but I never stopped wanting to be with my dad.

He had a new family by then, and they were living in Charlotte, North Carolina. I had started to come into my own as a football player around that time, though football was more of my father's idea than my own. I became a pretty good defensive tackle at East Mecklenburg High School, where I was known as Dusty Runnels. Everyone knew who my dad was, in part because longtime professional wrestler Gene Anderson's son, Brad, was in the same school and played football, too. Both of us were far more passionate about wrestling than football or pretty much anything else outside of girls.

Prior to our junior season, we shaved our heads like the Road Warriors, Hawk and Animal. Every chance we had, Brad and I would do trampoline wrestling. We'd put on an entire show from start to finish. My girlfriend would videotape me pulling up to the house in my dad's Mercedes as if I were arriving at the arena. I'd wear my dad's robes. We'd have his replica title belts. We took time to create these elaborate setups, making the whole experience as real as possible. We each had our music playing as we came toward the trampoline, which was our ring.

I liked playing football, but I loved wrestling. I'm sure it had something to do with the idea of wanting to be with my dad. But he tried to keep me away from it, that's for sure. I probably should have taken a football scholarship, gone to college, and earned a degree, because then I would have had something to fall back on if wrestling didn't work out. Maybe that was my dad's thinking. All I know is that I was blinded by the desire to be a part of his life. The fact that it's such a hard life never entered my mind. All I know is that I had the fever.

Transitionwise, it wasn't a big deal for me to move from Austin to Charlotte. I was a big kid and an athlete, so I didn't have much trouble adjusting to a new school. But it was not what I expected. My dad was still gone much of the time. He is a great loving father and both of us have changed in so many ways over the years. But at the time, I wanted and needed him to be the nurturing kind of father. I thought everything was going to be exactly how I had pictured it all those years when I was living in Austin. I thought there would be more father-son time, more time to build a deeper relationship with him. Instead, he always seemed grumpy and grouchy, which I understand now. He was working a lot inside and outside the ring. He was doing double duty as the boss working with Jim Crockett Promotions at National Wrestling Alliance before it became World Championship Wrestling. He was booking the talent and pushing himself, which meant there were always guys pissed off at him for one reason or another. Some guys were unhappy because they weren't working enough.

Other guys were mad that someone else was getting pushed ahead of them. He had to hire and fire guys. That's the way it worked. He had the heat coming down from the wrestlers, but he couldn't cater to every person because he was pushing himself, too. He also was a huge star at the time. He was the American Dream, Dusty Rhodes. He was as big as anyone in professional wrestling. My dad had to be creative and tough at the same time because he knew how to draw crowds and make money. If a guy wasn't on the same page, then he had to get rid of him. I'm sure he created enemies along the way. As hard as it had to be physically, the mental stress of working both ends of the business had to be exhausting.

Dad pushing himself to the limit.

I didn't mind playing football, because he wanted me to play. Besides, I thought I'd be playing in front of my father every week. As it turned out, I hardly got to see him. When I did see him he was riding me about homework, girls, grades, or something else. It was a letdown, but I had my buddies, so life moved on.

Although I wanted nothing more than to follow my father into wrestling, he hadn't yet smartened me up. I played football and wrestled during my last two years in high school, and I did very well. Despite poor grades, I had a bunch of scholarship offers. Tennessee, Utah, and Louisville were among the schools that recruited me. I decided on the University of Louisville, where Howard Schnellenberger had taken over the program. But my heart wasn't in the game. I had my mind oriented in one direction. I wanted to follow in my dad's footsteps.

Back then professional wrestlers were very serious about keeping everything a secret. It was like a religion. There were a couple bosses I had early on who told us that if we went out drinking and got into a fight, we'd better not lose or we'd be fired. In my dad's time if you wrestled somebody, you couldn't be seen out partying with that guy later on. They would show up in separate cars and they never gave away their secrets. There were always people who thought they knew a little bit about what happened in the ring, though. I'd hear kids at school say, "Aw, wrestling's fake. Your father isn't really doing anything. It's all just fake." I hated that word then, and I still hate it today. It really annoys me when somebody calls what we do fake. And I kicked more than a little butt as I got older because of that word. But my dad kept it so quiet. All those guys at the time used to speak their own language. They called it "carny," and my dad and mother, then later my stepmother would discuss a match or something going on in the business in this language that only they and other wrestlers could understand. That's how protective they were of the business. They were serious about it in a way that's hard to imagine today. Over time I picked up the language and figured out what they were saying. Little by little I learned how to speak it as well. Now it's a lost art.

Rappers sing or perform in a kind of carny language of their own. I still talk in carny with some of the veterans because I love it. I don't know where it went, though. You talk carny to some of the young guys and they're like, "What is he talking about?" These young guys should know this stuff because it's part of the history of our business. That's the way we were raised, using carny language to communicate inside and outside the ring. It was like our own secret society and everyone followed the rules. It was great. Some of the bosses back then, if you got caught riding with a guy you were doing an angle with, they'd fire you on the spot. I kayfabed all the time. That is the art of keeping it all real for the fans by staying in character at all times. If I was driving with a guy I was wrestling that night, I'd jump out of the car down the road from the arena so we could keep the angle pure. I couldn't see doing it any other way. We took it very seriously. When Steve Austin and I had our run in the early 1990s, we were very cautious about being seen together. Today, guys who just wrestled on television are out having a beer together and no one thinks twice about it.

To this day I don't really know why my father was against me getting into professional wrestling. Obviously he knew how hard the life could be and maybe he wanted something different, something better for his son. I think that's why he pushed football so hard. But I didn't want to do anything else. Midway through my senior year in high school, my father moved back to Dallas. My little brother, Cody, was only a baby when they left, so I stayed behind and finished up my school year. Then I packed up what little I had and drove to Dallas.

By then my father knew I wasn't going to go to college to play football. He called me up one day and said, "Pick me up at the airport in Dallas. We have something to talk about." The airport was about a forty-five-minute drive from our new house in Texas. He got into my truck and launched into a forty-five-minute crash course on professional wrestling. He not only smartened me up about the way everything operates, but he covered the business outside the ring and beyond the arena. I took it all in. I probably knew by that point that the outcomes were set up in advance, but he explained how angles were developed. I remember being so impressed by his business sense and creativity. He understood every corner of it. He clued me in to some of the private verbiage wrestlers used, the carny language, between themselves in the ring so fans wouldn't understand.

"Tomorrow night I want you to be in Amarillo," he said. "First, go to a sporting goods store and buy yourself a referee shirt and some black cotton pants. You are going to referee two matches."

This was 1988 and I was nineteen years old. I did exactly as my father asked, stopping by the store, then driving 350 miles to Amarillo in my used red Jeep Comanche pickup. Everyone else, including my father, took a private jet. My dad wanted me to pay my dues, so I hit the road. He laid it all out in that speech. He told me that I had to work hard for anything I got. It was the first and only time he smartened me up about the business. He went through the whole deal and I just did what I was told.

In the second match I refereed, my pants split from the top of the front all the way around the back when I went down for the three-count. And there was nothing under there. I was holding up Rock-n-Roll Express's hands and my privates were hanging out. All the boys were at the curtain watching to see how I would do. I thought I did a pretty good job, but then I saw Tommy Young, the head referee at that time, pointing down at my crotch. There I was, holding up Rock-n-Roll Express's hands, and everything was just hanging out. I remember thinking, "Oh my God." I came back through the curtain and it was like I parted the Red Sea. Everyone was lying on the floor laughing like crazy. That was how I got my start. I had never even been in a wrestling ring before that night.

That night I took my dad to the airport so he could fly back to Dallas. He gave me a few bucks for gas and I drove the 365 miles back home.

I made $20 that night.

two

WRESTLING 101:
BUSINESS SCHOOL

The ride back from Amarillo was one of the easiest six-hour drives in my life. I didn't care what came next. I was ready to soak up the world I had spent my entire life thinking about.

When I returned home, my dad sent me to train with Jim Wehba, who was known as Skandor Akbar. My dad had known Skandor for years and he trusted him to teach me the basics at Doug's Gym in downtown Dallas. The place was bare-bones, to say the least. It had been a hard-core weight-lifting gym, but it was pretty much empty when I walked through the door for the first time. As you walked through the place and toward the back, there was a large cinder-block wall with a hole in it. Someone had literally just punched a hole through this wall. On the other side was an old broken-down boxing ring crammed into a small room. The floor of the ring was up on cinder blocks and there were no ropes. The walls were really close and the floor had no give whatsoever. We did a lot of mat wrestling initially. The first thing Skandor said was, "Take ten falls onto your back and get up as fast as you can." There were a couple other guys there, along with Jacqueline Moore, who later became a WWE Diva. Landing on that floor felt like falling onto a dirt field. I was sore as hell after that first day, but I loved every minute.

Skandor was in his mid-fifties at the time and had been around sports entertainment for years working for Bill Watts's Universal Wrestling Federation in the 1980s. He worked a lot of the regional territories with my father. I spent only a couple months with Skandor before my father sent me to Tampa to learn at the feet of Steve Keirn and Mike Graham. My father's mentor was Mike's dad, Eddie Graham. When Eddie was inducted into the WWE Hall of Fame in 2008 following his death, my dad accepted the award for him.

Mike was running Florida Championship Wrestling at the time, working out of the Sportatorium on Albany Street in Tampa. My dad sent me to Florida with $2,000 and my truck. I grabbed whatever clothes I had, put on my boots, and took off.

I lived with my stepmother's sister and worked the Florida territory for two years and got $20 a night. If I was lucky, I'd find a photographer to take pictures and we'd sell those inside the building for gas and beer money. I'm sure my father was watching and paying attention to how I was doing, but I didn't know that at the time. Mike, being his mentor's son, was no doubt on the phone with my father and keeping him updated on my progress. But I was having the time of my life. That was probably the most fun I have ever had in my life.

The first couple months I trained at the Sportatorium, where we had shows every Thursday night. The offices were upstairs in the same building and that's where I would go to train a couple hours every day. Other than that, I lived with my aunt and went out drinking every single night. The training schedule amounted to Steve or Mike telling me what time to show up every day. I was there to learn everything, including the psychology of performing in front of people. I took it all in. I just soaked up every ounce of information. Back then, though, I never went to the gym and worked out. I hated the gym. Very few guys really worked out seriously. Ironically, it's only been the last year and a half that I've come to love working out. I lift and train now to the point that it's become an obsession. Something that I hated so much when I was younger and naturally in great shape is what I crave now. I've lost fifty-six pounds in eighteen months, and I'm in the best shape of my life.

Mark Starr, who started out at the same time, was probably the only one who really trained hard. What training we did was at bars. We worked and drank, and a lot of nights we partied until the sun came up. I had no money, but I was home every night or morning, whichever came later.

We'd load up and drive to wherever we had to be for that night's show. Orlando was easy because I could get there and back on a tank of gas. No one had any money, so a hotel was pretty much out of the question. Gas wasn't expensive in 1988, so a couple of us would drive together and split the costs. We had an event every night—Tampa, Sarasota, Ft. Myers, St. Petersburg, Miami, Jacksonville.

Once a month we'd go to Nassau, Bahamas, for a couple days. There was a little bar we went to called Club Waterloo. We always had a good time, but in those days you kind of had to sleep with one eye open, if you know what I mean. Everyone would try to screw with you, particularly if you were the first one to pass out. You always had to worry about waking up with your head shaved, or missing a big chunk of an eyebrow. Sometimes you woke up with really awful crap written all over your body with a permanent marker. They might shred your pants. Those ribs were really fun.

There were a lot of guys learning the ropes the same way I was in those days. The Nasty Boys were around when I was in Tampa. There were a lot of guys I worked with at that time who were good enough to have made it big. For whatever reason, politics or timing, most of them didn't make it very far. But a lot of those guys really deserved more than they got, that's for sure. Guys like Mark Starr and Jimmy Backlund taught me a lot, and they deserved a bigger profile.

It was a lot of fun. I was doing exactly what I wanted to be doing and I was having the time of my life. There were a few fights along the way, and I wasn't shy about throwing down. If somebody started in about how wrestling was fake, or said something about my dad, then I would go. I remember walking across the street from a wedding reception to a local bar. I saw this kid in the parking lot but I didn't pay much attention until I got closer. He said, "Hey, Dustin Rhodes. Your dad's a fat piece of crap." I didn't say a word and I barely changed my pace. I walked right up to him and just dropped him with one punch. His girlfriend started swinging at me. She was screaming and making a scene while the guy was flat on his ass. I kept right on walking toward the entrance to the bar. Fred Ottman, a huge guy who went by Tugboat and by Typhoon (of the Natural Disasters) in WWE for a long time, was the bouncer at the bar that day. He also was marrying one of my aunts, so I was good to go there.

Just as I was getting to the door, another guy came rushing out. He was every inch as big as Fred, but this guy was a jacked weight lifter. He was at least six three and probably close to three hundred pounds, just a massive human being.

He looked like a killer. He had gold chains all around his neck and he was angry. I had suspenders on and a white shirt that now had a splatter of blood on it from the first guy I decked. The guy said, "Did you just hit my brother?" I thought, "This guy is big." He kept talking, getting louder and louder, the veins on his neck getting bigger and bigger. Then he turned his head and I just popped him. I dropped him with one punch, but I knew he wouldn't stay down, so I jumped down and just kept drilling him. By the time Fred arrived, I had one of the guy's gold chains broken off in my hand. I hurt my hand hitting him. He had a head like cement. Fred grabbed me and took me into the bar so I could calm down. Turns out Fred worked out with the guy at a local weight lifters' gym. He said, "Dustin, if he ever sees you, he's going to kill you." I got really lucky because there were a lot of times I could have been stabbed or killed. That was no doubt one of them.

You knew there were guys out there who wanted to see how tough you really were. It happened to me. But I got some very good fatherly advice early on. My dad said, "Always be the bigger man and walk away because people are going to talk shit about me and you. Just walk away from it." I didn't walk away very often when I was young, but I eventually figured out better ways to deal with those situations.

Another night, I met the party queen of Tampa in a nightclub. She was thirty-eight years old. I was nineteen and I thought I had fallen in love. She was putting it on me. She was teaching me stuff I didn't even know existed. For about two weeks I was mesmerized by everything about her. I never failed to show up for work because I loved what I did. But I was out every night all night. We'd drink at crazy bars all over town. I didn't have a care in the world—no children, no wife, no girlfriends, no rent. I was shacked up in her house for two weeks going out with her every night. Finally a week went by and Mike said, "Dustin, you've got to call your aunt. She's worried about you." I said, "Okay, whatever." Another week went by and I finally decided I should stop by to see my aunt. Now, my aunt comes from a Cuban family. They have their wild, loud, and scary side and I saw it all that day. My aunt came to the door, and she went to town on me and kicked me the hell out.

So I moved all my stuff, which wasn't a whole lot of anything, into the Sportatorium. I used Mike Graham's upstairs office as living quarters because I still wasn't making enough money to afford real rent. Every once in a while we'd get $40 for an event in Tampa if we did really well, but mostly it was still $20 a night. It was a struggle just getting to and from the events because no one was making any money. I had a lot of my stuff stolen out of the Sportatorium during my time there. My truck was broken into a few times. Mike would come to work and I'd be out cold in his office with the door locked. I'd usually just gotten in from the night before. Like I said, the ribs, jokes, and pranks wrestlers played on one another back then were unbelievable. I can thank Mike, though, for saving my eyebrows. He told everyone, "Dustin's eyebrows are not to be touched. That's an order coming from his dad."

Then one day it all ended. Mike called me up to his office and said, "Dustin, your dad wants you to go up to the National Wrestling Alliance."

I wasn't ready to go. I might have been ready to take the next step, but I was having way too much fun. I'd learned a lot and I was getting better all the time. But I didn't want the fun to end.

"No, I don't want to go, Mike. What are you talking about? I want to stay here."

Mike said he'd never seen anybody who wanted to stay in Florida making no money, particularly somebody living in the office of an old arena. I was barely twenty years old. I was going to go be tag-team partners with Kendall Windham (the brother of Barry Windham, who was a top star) as the Texas Broncos.

I pulled my few possessions together and climbed back into my truck for another drive into a new life, this one in Atlanta. But I was a mess. I really didn't have any clothes because I barely needed them in the life I was leading in Tampa. Half the time one of the pranks wrestlers played on one another was to rip up your clothes. When I got to

Atlanta, I looked terrible. My father took me to a mall and bought me some decent clothes so I didn't embarrass him or myself.

I learned a lot and I made a lot more money, like $100,000, but otherwise the NWA experience wasn't nearly as memorable as my time in Tampa. I went from sleeping in the office of a sports venue with raggedy clothes to having real money and a real career. But I also lived an often-repeated story. I didn't respect the money. If I had $1 in my pocket, then I'd try to spend $2. I traveled all over the United States for about a year as part of the Texas Broncos. Barry Windham remains one of the most important teachers I have had. I learned a lot from just watching him.

My dad always told me that some of my movements looked just like Barry's. He was a great worker. I guess Kendall never really got the push the way Barry did. Kendall could work, but that's just how it goes. One guy makes it over another and sometimes it has more to do with timing than anything else. I don't know why Kendall didn't get that push or didn't realize his potential, because he was a natural, just like Barry.

Then again, my dad was a natural, too. And as far as I was concerned it was just as natural for me to follow in his footsteps.

THREE

STEPPING INTO MY FATHER'S BOOTS

My dad never stuck out his hand and said, "Here, son, let me pull you to the top." He knew how hard it is and there wasn't much he could do to help if I didn't help myself. That's why he did everything in his power to dissuade me from becoming a professional wrestler. But when he realized that I wasn't going to do anything else and that I loved it, he made sure I received the right direction from the right people.

But there were no shortcuts. If my dad had anything to do with it, then I had to earn anything and everything that came my way. That was the best approach, no question about it. Bill Watts pushed his son, Erik, too fast in WCW and both of them took a lot of heat for not going slower. It wasn't Erik's fault. He just wanted to get to the top. But he wasn't ready, and I was able to see that experience first-hand. Here's the boss's son, so okay, he's going to get a little more push than the next guy. When he's not ready, though, the other guys have very little tolerance, and a lot of them weren't too happy about it. Ultimately, I don't know if the heat got to Erik, or why he never made it as big as he probably wanted. Everybody knew I was one of the bosses' sons, too. No one knew that better than me. But other than being around my dad, I didn't want any favors. I was a stud in those days, and I wasn't afraid of doing whatever I had to do—on my own—to get to where I wanted to be. Did it help that Dusty Rhodes was my father? Sure. But I worked my butt off and I loved every minute of it.

For a long time I was comfortable being in the shadow of my dad. I was happy just trying to get into his shoes. So when my dad left the NWA for WWE, I was more than happy to follow him there a few months later.

Vince McMahon wanted to take a look at me, so I had what they called a tryout with journeyman Black Bart. Bart led me through the match, and I did fine. So Vince hired me and I started working on an angle with my father. I always wanted to wrestle with my dad, but he never did. He was wrestling Randy "Macho Man" Savage and he was fixing to start something with Ted DiBiase, the Million Dollar Man. They had me in the front row next to the ring like I was watching the match. This was my first big-time shoot and it was huge. I was sitting there cheering for my dad when Ted and his bodyguard, Virgil, came out. They started handing $100 bills to everybody in the front row so they could take all the seats and get the fans out of the way. They wanted to buy my seat, too, but I wouldn't take the money. Ted sat to one side of me and Virgil on the other as I watched my father in the ring. Every time I stood up, they yanked me back down into my chair, which was one of those old wooden folding chairs. Ted handed me the money and I crumpled it up before throwing it into Virgil's face.

Then all of a sudden, I turned around and hit Ted. I was a big guy, in great shape at the time. It was just really cool to be interacting with all these guys and my dad in a big event. I also had this mullet going, long bleached-blond hair. Then I hit Virgil, and Ted reached over and clotheslined me over the rail. My dad was doing his thing in the ring, so he hadn't realized what was happening yet. Then Teddy picked up one of the wooden chairs and hit me square in the head with the corner. It was the first time I was really busted open. *Boom*, he hit me with a straight-on shot and I went down. I was bleeding like crazy and wondering, "Was that supposed to happen?"

My dad came running out of the ring. He was screaming, "Oh, my God!" He was selling it so well for the camera that it was amazing. He knew exactly how to pull it off to maximum effect. I watched him, almost as if it was in slow motion, and marveled at how good he was at selling the moment. To this day, I don't know if they planned that without telling me. Back then you never knew with those guys. I ended up with a few stitches. So what? I loved it. We ended up having a tag-team match with my dad and me against Ted and Virgil at the Royal Rumble in Miami.

In between, the Million Dollar Man had an angle going with my father and me. Ted would tell my dad, "I can beat your son's ass in ten minutes or less," but he couldn't do it, so that really set me up. Ted was a great teacher.

Soon after the Royal Rumble my dad left WWE. I wanted to do the same for no other reason than to be with him. My father wanted to go back to Florida to open up Professional Wrestling Federation under his name and management. He wanted to get it back to where it had been in the old days. So I asked Vince for my release. It wasn't a hard decision personally or professionally. When I decided to leave, Vince told my father, "You take him right now, Dusty, but one of these days I'm going to steal Dustin back and make a star out of him."

I learned early on that Vince is a genius. He could make a star out of a stick of chewing gum. When it comes to virtually any aspect of the business, Vince is unbelievable. Still, I didn't know if I'd ever work for Vince again. I was just going with the flow, and the flow took me back to Tampa.

My dad was running the show back in Florida and I had proved myself during the brief runs at NWA and the World Wrestling Federation. So he made me the Florida Heavyweight Champion. I was having fun, but it wasn't the same compared to my earlier days in Tampa. I still wanted to be as big as my dad. That desire was as strong as ever and I worked as hard as I could to make that happen.

At the time, though, I was still in his shadow and that was fine by me. In terms of money, returning to Florida was an economic step back, but so what? I loved being with my dad. I was twenty-one years old with no ties, no commitments, and very few bills. It might not have been as much fun as the first time around, but I was living a little better. I had very few complaints.

At one point my dad sent me to Japan for a month. It was my first trip to Japan and I had no idea what to expect. For some guys, a month over there is a long time. I had heard so many stories about guys cracking over there because everything, even the wrestling, was so totally foreign. But I loved it. It was a different style, unbelievably different. Wresting of any kind has always been huge in Japan. Everyone knows about sumo wrestling, but the Japanese are passionate about professional wrestling, too. Even the sumo wrestlers came to our matches over there.

I was paid $1,500 a week in Japan, which was huge because I was there for a month. The food was the only thing I hated about Japan. Thank God for McDonald's and the Hard Rock Cafe. I ate at McDonald's every day.

Japanese crowds are very old school. They are very quiet and proper, almost to the point of being weird.

There would be seventy thousand people in the stands and you could hear a cricket. There would be collective *oohs* and *aahs*, but otherwise they were stone silent. American fans are crazy. They're drinking, screaming, and behind the match from the opening minute. In Japan, a big move would produce a loud sigh and some very controlled clapping. Then they would shut up again and watch. Toward the end of the match, when you have a series of close falls and a guy kicks out, that's when they started to get into it.

The Japanese wrestlers were into keeping it real, known as kayfabe-ing, for the fans. Everything was very secretive, even more than it was in the States back then. Before the show you couldn't even talk to the guy you were going to wrestle. The referee would go back and forth between dressing rooms relaying information, which made everything a lot more difficult. They spoke very little English, but enough that I could understand what they wanted me to do in the ring.

We were stars over there because of how big wrestling was in general. A guy like me, six four with blond hair, really stood out. In those early trips to Japan, they didn't necessarily know who I was, but they would stop and stare at me. They knew my dad because he had been over there probably a couple dozen times over the years. As the years went on, they knew I was Dusty Rhodes Jr., which is what

I was always called in Japan. I enjoy the country, or anywhere overseas, for that matter.

There is a big difference between a live show and a television show. Everything moves so much faster on television. You have very little time to set up the match. A live event is much different in terms of time and what you can do. At a live event, the opening match might go twelve minutes and you can tell a story out there.

I try to focus on that one person in the front row who I know doesn't want to be there. I find him, too, because there is always somebody who comes to the match because his son or daughter is a big fan. That dad isn't interested. He hates wrestling, and you can see it on his face. "This stuff sucks. It's fake. I can't wait to get out of here." I can see the kids are jumping up and down as the dad sits there hating every one of those first few minutes. Then, after a move or two I start to see a little bit of a sparkle, a barely visible twinkle in his eyes. Still, he's not there yet. He isn't even close to getting out of his seat, much less getting emotionally involved in the match. When I see that first glimmer in his eyes I know he's starting to pay attention to what's happening in the ring. I do a couple more moves. Maybe I get slammed in a way that looks like the other guy has killed me. I look over again, this time I can see the look in his eyes change. He's focused on the ring now. He's wondering, "Can this crazy guy with the face paint even stand up after that? That looked real." The dad looks over at his son or daughter, who is either near tears or in tears because I'm getting the crap kicked out of me ten feet away. They look to their father, "Is he okay, Daddy?" Now I'm conscious of directing every action, every fall toward this guy. I'll go right over to the ropes near his seat and make sure he sees the emotion on my face. The guy is cradling his kid, who is still in tears. And I know what he's thinking: "This guy is really hurt. He needs some help out there." I know that's going through his mind because now he's looking around. Is somebody going to go into the ring and help that guy? Is there a doctor approaching? Then his eyes change again. Now they start to light up. I begin to make a comeback. The kid stops crying. The dad can't believe I might be able to get to my feet. I move my shoulders a little bit, shake the cobwebs out of my head, and slowly come up to one knee. The dad isn't out of his seat yet, but he's fixated on what's happening in the ring. His kid is starting to see some hope. Then I start whipping the other guy's butt. I'm on fire. The next thing I know, the dad and the kid are out of their seats. Both of them are screaming now. Everybody in the arena is on his or her feet screaming.

My goal was to get that one guy onto his feet. I needed him to believe that what he was seeing was real. When he got off his chair, that's when I knew I did my job that night. I lived for those moments.

When we went back down to Florida, my dad ran every-thing. I was his son and he took care of me, but nothing was easy. Eventually my dad went back to WCW and I went my own way for a while. I hooked up with the United States Wrestling Association out of Tennessee. I worked that territory with Jerry Jarrett, Jeff Jarrett, Jerry Lawler, and some other guys for eight months to a year.

There were a lot of guys who helped me along the way. Mike Graham and Steve Keirn taught me how to work and hone my trade during those years in Florida. Then I was fortunate to get hooked up with guys like Barry Windham, Arn Anderson, Bobby Eaton, and Larry Zbyszko. Those guys taught me the nitty-gritty of professional wrestling. A lot of my work is like Barry's. He is so smooth and so good. Thanks to what I learned from Barry, I work smooth as well. Arn, Bobby, and Larry were guys who did things the right way. They paid attention to detail and they were passionate about the business. Those guys all made me a bigger star than I was at the time simply because they were so good and they cared about what they were doing. They knew how to work the crowd and at the same time they were taking a kid like me to the next level. Ricky Steam-boat taught me how to get beat up. It might not sound that difficult, but there is a fine art to showing people you are in pain and being able to completely sell that emotion. He taught me when to move, when to stay down on the mat, when to show my face, and how to do it in the most convincing manner.

When I wrestled with Arn or Ricky Steamboat, sometimes we would go for an hour. We did that several times. One night at the Omni in Atlanta, we went for nearly an hour and we never lost the fans. Arn, Ricky, and Bobby were just that good. They knew how to operate in the ring, how to tell a story and keep it compelling for sixty minutes. They were remarkable. They didn't run around the ring trying to take time off the clock. Those guys worked.

That night Ricky and I were fighting Bobby Eaton and Arn Anderson, who were the Tag-Team Champions at the time. It was a live event and the Omni was sold out. Since there wasn't any television, we were supposed to go an hour and end the match in a draw. As I said, those guys were so good that I wasn't worried about anything. With about ten minutes left in the match, I was blown sky high. By that I mean that I was sucking wind in a way that felt like I was having a heart attack. I couldn't catch my breath. I was huffing and puffing, gasping for air.

Both Arn and Bobby were looking at me like, "What is wrong with this kid? Is he dying or something?" Meanwhile, I was freaking out. Literally, I couldn't breathe. I couldn't get any air. It probably looked like I was dying because that's pretty much how I felt. We had spent so much time building up to the final tag that I was spent.

At about the eight-minute mark, Arn said, "You guys are going to win the title tonight." We switched the planned finish over the last few minutes because I had freaked out. That was the first time I had ever gone beyond twenty-five or thirty minutes in a match, and I was blown out by all the work. The guys were looking at one another, tagging in and out saying, "What's wrong with this guy? What's going on?" They would look at me and say, "Just breathe. Take a breath." Then I'd scream back, "I can't. I can't breathe. Oh, my God." It felt like I was being suffocated. Finally somebody said, "Just do something." That's when I rolled over and tagged with Ricky. At that point I knew what they were thinking. "Now what are we going to do? We have built up a hell of a match and Dustin just screwed up the whole thing." They had to improvise and let us win at that point because we had every person in the Omni on their feet. They were ready for us to win the title and we couldn't let them down. When the match ended and we all got back behind the curtain, the guys said, "What happened to you, man?" They weren't upset or anything like that. We had a really good match, which was all they cared about. Ending it the way we did was probably the best outcome possible for the fans.

I don't know how they did it, though. I don't know if I could have done it without them. I've always believed you are only as good as the other person in the ring with you.

And they made me better, no question about it. I'm not saying it's a lost art, but those guys were different.

Steve Austin was in the same mold. When my dad was back in control at WCW, he brought me in. That's when I got my first big push. Steve was there at the time and we had some tremendous matches working together in the early 1990s. He was Stunning Steve Austin and I was the Natural, and man, we tore down some houses. We had wars. We were young, highly motivated, and totally committed to what we were doing. We'd go out and do twenty to twenty-five minutes a night. Either he was the United States Champion or I was, and we weren't afraid to try something new because we absolutely loved what we were doing. All we cared about was walking away knowing we had a great match. We knew the fans were pleased with us, but we were also pleased because of the effort and skill we put into those matches.

I met Steve at the USWA. We were two guys from Texas just going for it all the time. It was old-school wrestling. We had the same attitude because we had been taught the right way. We were tearing it up night after night and having a hell of a time along the way.

One night we were in Phoenix for a match. Lex Luger and Sting were really hot at the time, and they were there, too. I was the United States Champion working with Steve. Grizzly Smith, Jake "the Snake" Roberts's dad, was the road agent. I love Grizzly. What a good man. Austin and I were talking about the match and what we were going to do that night. Now, this was a bought-and-paid-for show at the local fair. So the audience was made up of wrestling fans, but there were also people coming to the show because they just happened to be at the fair that day. None of that mattered to Austin and me. We didn't care whether there were ten people in the stands or ten thousand. We were all about tearing down the house every time we stepped into the ring.

Steve and I knew how to work. We could grab hold of the audience from the opening minute and have them the entire way. Steve was a natural. We exchanged ideas, but most of the time he called the match. Sometimes I'd call something out in the middle of a match, and Steve would go with it. We worked really smooth. It was like ballet in the ring when we were together. He is a good guy, just a good old boy.

I was just doing my job and keeping my nose clean, literally. I wasn't doing any drugs or anything else other than drinking. I was still in my early twenties and was learning from the best. I didn't do a program with Rick Rude the way I did with Steve, but Rick was another guy who helped me tremendously. He had that old-school savvy and he helped, no question about it. Everything was going pretty well, though my demons were circling. I just didn't notice.

Around that time I started recognizing the fact I really

Wrestling Vader in my WCW days.

was in my dad's shadow. The more successful I became, the more obvious it was to me. I started getting weighed down by the idea that I was never going to be my own person, that I was always going to be Dusty's kid. Sure, I did well, but I knew people thought my success was due in part, in large part according to some, to being Dusty's son.

It didn't help matters that I had all kinds of insecurities. No matter how well I was doing, my father never really articulated how he felt about me or my performance. It wasn't until later in my career that he would say, "Good job" or "I'm proud of you, son." He'd tell me he loved me, but I needed to know how he felt about me as a wrestler. I wanted his approval just like every son wants his father's approval. He was the boss, and I understood that, but I also was his son. There didn't need to be any office politics between us, just some affirmation. "Tell me how you feel," I wanted to say. "Tell me I'm doing a good job. Tell me you are proud of me." I never really knew how well I was doing. As a result, I was always very critical of myself. To this day I can't watch myself on television. All I see are the flaws. I became very self-conscious about my performances. I'm insecure about a lot of things, so self-doubt came naturally. I've had to figure out life by myself, but in a lot of ways that experience didn't make me a stronger person. To the contrary, figuring out where I fit and how I measured up with my dad made me weaker in a lot of ways because I always questioned myself. I am still very hard on myself. I'm a perfectionist. I could have used some words of encouragement or support from my father along the way.

I guess the fact is that while I might have been performing in front of twenty thousand people and millions more on television, I was looking for the approval of only one person. And as time went on I realized I needed to step out of my father's boots and go out on my own. There's never been a day when I haven't been proud of the Rhodes name and the family legacy established by my father.

But I needed to breathe a little in a space I created.

FOUR

THE LONG GOODBYE

It wasn't long after I started thinking about the weight of my father's shadow that my life took a turn. I guess that's how it works, but I never saw it coming.

I met my first wife, Terri, at WCW. She was a makeup artist for CNN. I was attracted to Terri the first time I laid eyes on her. We finally got together in Phoenix, where I was in town for a show. I had gone golfing during that day and I returned to the hotel and headed down to the bar to have a drink with my dad, which was ironic, given everything that followed.

Terri was in the bar with Dad and others, and she was the hottest woman I had ever seen. She was so damn sexy that I couldn't keep my eyes off her. Even to this day I can't pinpoint exactly what it was that attracted me to her. She was beautiful, but there was that extra something about Terri. We talked and drank all night at the bar. I was on my best behavior, being respectful and as nice as possible. I was smitten, that's for sure. When the night started winding down and it was time for her to go up to her room, I walked her up. I had every desire, but no intention of sleeping with her that night. Not that I was necessarily in control of that decision. I helped her into bed, covered her up, and went on my way.

The strategy worked to perfection. The next day she thought I had been a complete gentleman, which of course was true. That's when it all started between us. Initially, we were seeing one another behind everyone's back, trying to keep it quiet. We both had careers and it just seemed keeping things quiet was the right approach. Eventually we became very involved and moved in together. After about six months, I took Terri to Austin to meet my mother. At that point I still didn't think my dad knew about our relationship. I was just going about my business, doing my job and spending more and more time with Terri. But no secret lasts very long in the world we were in.

On the way back home from Texas and that time with my mother, I received a page in the airport. We were fixing to get on the plane and head back home when I heard my name. Anyone who's ever flown knows the message: Pick up the nearest courtesy phone. I walked over, picked up the phone, and it was my dad. He started right in telling me all kinds of things about Terri. I was caught completely off guard because I didn't think he knew about us, much less anything about Terri personally. He had been fine around her at the bar in Phoenix, and as far as I knew he didn't have an opinion about her one way or another.

"Do you know where she's been?" he asked. It went downhill from there. "You need to get home, straighten out, and think right." The conversation didn't last long, but my father, as always, got my attention. I didn't know whom I was angrier with, Terri or my dad. I hung up the phone, walked onto the plane, and started taking it out on Terri. I blamed her for every bit of anger I felt, for having to endure a lecture from my father. I was so mean that I made her cry all the way home.

But it wasn't her fault. It didn't take much for my insecurities to come out, especially when my father was involved. I loved Terri and I loved my father. He didn't make it an ultimatum or anything like that, and I'm sure he was just looking out for his son. As time went on he mentioned a couple other things to me about Terri, but I just blew them off. As far as I was concerned, it was my life and he was going to have to deal with it.

Over time, my dad became more accepting, but every time he said something negative about Terri, it touched a nerve with me. Finally, we got to the point that we'd go to family outings together. She didn't like to go because there was always an uncomfortable feeling in the air. She'd show up with me, and my father seemed to come around to the fact that she wasn't going away.

When Terri became pregnant with our daughter, Dakota, we got married and everything was fine. I was still working at WCW, and my dad was still there, too. Life was about as normal as you could expect. Dakota was like a gift from heaven, a little girl beautiful in ways I couldn't have imaged before she was born.

One day, my dad called and asked me to play golf. He lived about an hour away from us in Marietta, Georgia. We agreed to meet at a little store in a strip mall not far from our house.

Just as I hung up the phone, Terri told me she wasn't feeling well. We had this little baby who needed to be taken of and Terri was so sick that she wanted me to cancel the golf outing.

"Please don't go today," she said. "I'm really sick, Dustin. I need your help with the baby. I need you here today."

What could I do? I knew my father wouldn't be happy, but given the circumstances I figured he'd at least understand. Hell, he had kids. He knew that the unexpected happened. I went out into the car and drove up to the store where we were supposed to meet. I told him I couldn't play and that Terri was at home sick. Those two facts pushed him over the edge. He was upset that he had driven an hour for nothing. And I'm sure the fact Terri was involved only made him angrier. It didn't end well, to say the least. Maybe he felt like I picked Terri over him. I don't know. But that was the last time I spoke to him for five years.

I have no idea how the door just slams shut between two people like that. Yet it's ironic in a way. All the pain I felt from our estrangement led to some of my greatest professional success. Maybe I needed that distance. I don't know, but it was a tough time for both of us.

Dakota remained in my father's life, but he and my stepmother were barely able to see her from that point. I didn't speak to him and I didn't see him, which might be remarkable given the business we were in. Before long, the weight of it all became too heavy for me to control. Soon after, I started going to therapy hoping to find a way to deal with the situation. In fact, Terri and I were both going. I spent all this money trying to find a way around the pain, but nothing helped. My dad called our place a couple times when I was out, and he talked to Terri. Small talk mostly. Why couldn't he call me? Why should I have to pick up the phone and call him? He was the one who stormed off and slammed the door on our relationship. I was supposed to make the first move because he's my dad? Out of respect? Where was his respect for his son? This was my wife, the mother of my daughter, and because there was a problem I couldn't play golf. Big deal.

This went on for five long, hard, and very tumultuous years with great highs and even greater lows. It was the hardest time of my life emotionally and psychologically. That's when I started getting deeper into the use of prescription painkillers and alcohol.

With my lifestyle, one injury can lead to another. I have an addictive personality and I was a mess emotionally—a volatile mix for someone like me. Add in the burden of trying to get out from under my father's shadow, and I was not in a good place.

I'd take the painkillers and then drink alcohol to medicate myself to get away from it all. The distance from my father was destroying me mentally, and to one degree or another it was contributing to me destroying myself physically. Terri would tell me I needed to call my father because she could see how his absence from my life was tearing me apart. Every time she mentioned my father, or talked about what I should do to repair the relationship, I exploded. I didn't have the tools to deal with the situation. All my insecurities were on hyperalert, and it was like I was paralyzed by anxiety.

More than once, Terri told me to grab a pen and a piece of paper so she could tell me what to say to my dad over the phone. I'd write it all down. Should I tell him that I'd meet him halfway? My dad has always been intimidating. Hell, he's still intimidating. I didn't have any idea what was going on in his mind, so mine ran wild.

After a couple months, I finally got myself to the point where I could pick up the phone and call him. I told him not to say a word, just to listen. I told him the way it was with Terri and me, and if he wanted to meet me halfway to discuss this, or fight me, then I'd meet him halfway. Then I just hung up. *Click.* From that point on, we didn't communicate. He was very receptive, but . . . I don't know. I could tell that he was really sad on the other end of that call.

I had always wanted nothing more than to be a part of my dad's life, to make him proud and earn his approval. Then, in a moment I never saw coming, he disappeared. He was gone, out of my life all over again. As time went on, there didn't seem to be any hope of ever bridging the gap between us. It led to me becoming verbally abusive with Terri because I didn't have the tools or the emotional maturity to see myself through all the pain. Terri and I started down the road to divorce at about the five-year mark of an eight-year marriage.

The next cut hurt less, at least physically. I was fired by the WCW for blading. I knew it was against WCW rules. It was in the script and I actually questioned whether or not we could do it on the bus ride to a shoot. I told the head producer, "For whatever reason, WCW boss Eric Bischoff doesn't want us to blade. We need to get this approved from up above." I didn't want to blade because I knew the consequences. Sure enough, the producer told us we had approval from the higher-ups. I still wasn't comfortable, but what the hell. I didn't have a problem with blading. I just didn't want to get fired for it.

The shoot took place in north Georgia. I drove up from where I lived, south of Atlanta. There were two tour buses parked on this farm where Barry Darsow and I dressed and prepared for the shoot. And there was an eighteen-wheeler that had been outfitted with a giant cage on the bed. The setup was elaborate. Inside the cage were small cameras to film the fight. There were weapons—farm tools—that we used to beat up one another. At the very far end of the trailer was a post with a bell on it. One of us had to climb up the side of the cage to get to the post. Whoever rang the bell first won the match. All of this happened while the truck was driving down the road. This was a Blacktop Bully match and that was the rationale for having an eighteen-wheeler involved. The cops shut down a couple miles of the road, and off we went.

It took us twenty or twenty-five minutes to shoot the whole thing. We were throwing one another against the cage, grabbing the weapons and anything we could get our hands on to use on one another. About halfway through the match, we started blading. Meanwhile the truck was driving down the road with two four-wheel-drive trucks on either side with cameras. The cage was pretty strong. It wasn't like we were going to fall off anything, but there were some curves. When we saw a curve coming up, we'd fall hard into the turn. Most of what we did in that match was done on the fly because we didn't get a chance to drive the road before the shoot. It ended with us returning to the farmhouse. I chased Barry out of the truck and tackled him in a ditch. We were fighting covered in mud. It was fun and I felt really good about the shoot. That's why what happened the next day was such a shock. I didn't see it coming. None of us saw it coming.

Mike Graham, who was an agent, and I drove back to Atlanta together. It was just another routine day at the office. The next day, Mike called and said they had let him go. "Be prepared, Dustin, because you're probably going to get a call, too." Sure enough, the call came.

There were a lot of people coming into the company at the time, some of them with huge salaries. I've always thought they trumped up the whole thing so they could move some money around and take care of some other people.

I never would have done something that I knew to be against company policy. I'm a businessman first. I told Eric, "I did what I was told to do." I brought up the fact that our booking sheets made clear we were supposed to follow any directions by the agents. I told him a call had been made, but Eric didn't bend.

"We've got to let you go, Dustin."

I was making a good salary at the time. I could have taken legal action, but that would have cost me time and money. I didn't know what I was doing one way or another at that point, so I just let it set. As it turned out, that was the best decision I could have made because Eric took care of me down the road.

In that moment nothing about the future mattered. My life was starting to spin a little faster than I could control.

But against all odds and reason, the best time of my career was right around the corner.

FİVE

THE MAIN EVENT

The demons were circling. I knew I hadn't done anything wrong. It came out of the blue, just like the fallout with my dad, with no warning. I couldn't have imagined being let go, because wrestling was the one thing holding my life together.

Meanwhile, I was home living off what I had in the bank, which wasn't much. There were constant household issues around paying the bills. I was taking more and more pills trying to dull the pain of everything swirling around in my head. I had no idea what the future held, but I had no thought of going out and getting a regular job.

I'm an entertainer. Even when I retire I want to stay connected to wrestling. I definitely want to help the up-and-coming future stars, something—anything—to stay connected.

I had been out of work for about eight months when Vince McMahon called me.

"Dustin, are you sitting down?"

"Yes, sir."

I was excited and nervous at the same time because Vince is very intimidating. Vince and Bruce Prichard were both on the line. Bruce was a former commentator who went by the name Brother Love and he was part of Vince's brain trust at the time. Vince said, "I've got this character I want to run by you. His name is Goldust." Bruce kind of filled in the blanks. They said Goldust was an androgynous character. I knew what that meant, even though they never said, or even implied, that Goldust was gay. To this day, they have never used that word in reference to Goldust. They just called him a bizarre, androgynous character.

When they finished I thought, "Oh, my God, what is this?"

After the call, I thought about the whole idea and realized Goldust could be the way for me to step out of my father's shoes and forever move myself out from under his shadow. This was a chance to do something on my own, and I knew it was going to make him angry all over again. That fact pushed me toward Goldust even more because we weren't in a good place and I didn't really give a damn at that point. Mostly, I wanted to do something outside the Rhodes name. I love that name. It's my heritage and my family, but I wanted to do something that was mine alone.

The more Vince explained the character, the more attracted to the idea I became. I've always been fascinated with paint. Basically, I would look like a gold statue, like an Oscar with some bizarre things painted onto my face. At the very beginning, it was just a gold-painted face with two black-painted eyes and ears. Nothing else. Vince brought me up to Stamford several times to talk about the character. He said, "We want to make you a heel, a bad guy." I'd never been a bad guy. In all my years of working to that point, I'd always been a babyface, a good guy. The idea of becoming a heel was kind of nerve-racking because I knew I had a lot to learn. But Vince put me on the road right away.

The rift in my relationship with my father was going on at the same time I was about to do a character that was 180 degrees from my father's personality. I'm pretty sure that even if we had been talking at that time, I would have agreed to do Goldust because the weight of my father's shadow was becoming so heavy for me. Having to live up to his expectations probably would have eventually led me to do something as crazy as Goldust.

I heard through the grapevine that he hated the character, which wasn't surprising. I would dress up as certain people, and one time I dressed up like my father in polka dots. I'm sure that touched a nerve on a couple fronts. My dad had always been part of the competition prior to going to work for Vince the first time. He needed the work and

Vince brought him into what was World Wrestling Federation. The polka dots were Vince's idea, and my dad always thought it was an attempt to make fun of him. The idea was that my dad was the common man, a blue-collar kind of guy. Until that time, Pops had always been the boss. He had been at WCW when the two companies were fighting it out. I know it was hard for my dad to go to work for Vince, but he didn't have many choices at that time. He was Dusty Rhodes, but he wasn't the American Dream. They put Sapphire with him. I don't know whether everyone at World Wrestling Federation thought the whole deal with the polka-dot shirts and tights was funny, or whether it was a not-so-subtle jab at my dad. But my dad got over just like he always did. That's around the time I started the angle with Ted DiBiase and Randy "Macho Man" Savage, which also turned out to be Vince's first look at me.

I did all my dad's mannerisms as Goldust and then did an interview where I pretty much berated my father. That was a low blow. But I didn't really care at that point. I was just trying to play a character and entertain. The pain of our estrangement was so intense that it was almost kind of a distraction for me. This character was larger than life. I was making money and I was proud of myself for doing something on my own outside of the Rhodes name.

Vince told me Goldust was perfect for me. He had a

very clear idea of Goldust's characteristics and how he should look. It was like a cross-dresser wearing a robe and wig in a gold suit. The wig is a touchy subject with me even to this day. I wear the wig now because it's my character and it's entertainment. But back then I was thinking, "Man, this is a little much." I knew how creative Vince was, so I just listened to him and had faith that everything he said would work out.

I did some serious stuff as Goldust, and there were many times Vince told me we had to pull it back a little. Here was this androgynous, cross-dressing country-western Texan. In a lot of ways, Vince filled a father role for me at the time. I'm sure he knew my dad and I were having problems. Maybe that's why he brought Goldust to me in the first place. But he warned me there could be problems with the character.

"Dustin, you're going to have some problems with some of the boys, but don't do anything crazy. I want you to call me."

I wondered if Vince hadn't come up with this character for me to take my dad down a notch. My dad had become larger with WWE than Dusty Rhodes had ever been in Florida or with WCW. Whatever the reason, I decided the take the opportunity and run with it, just like my dad would have. Only this time, I wanted to run right out of his shadow.

At first it all was a little overwhelming. I was very nervous because I didn't want the character to flop. I started thinking that maybe Vince was trying to put me down because he had an issue with the Rhodeses. All my insecurities were rising to the surface and making me crazy. But Vince never wavered. He kept saying, "Dustin, you are going to get a lot of trouble from the boys, the fans. Just call me and we'll talk about it."

I had no idea what he was talking about until it actually started to happen. He was very hands-on for the first six months to a year. I took every direction, and Vince helped me bring the character to life. In one of the first promos I did, Vince didn't like the way I was talking. He wanted something more. I tried different voices and finally we nailed it. I created a couple of catchphrases, and that was the breakthrough. "You will always remember the name of Goldust" and "You will never forget the name of Goldust." I don't know where those phrases came from. It wasn't scripted at all. Goldust was a real calm, freaky, weird, bizarre character, and I was getting more and more comfortable with him. I knew people were thinking and wondering what was going on. "This guy is wacko. That's Dustin Rhodes, what is that boy thinking?" It was awesome.

Vince never does anything halfway. He gave me an opportunity and helped me make as much out of it as I could.

Bringing the house down with Savio.

Throughout the first year he was right there with me. I was nervous as hell, but he'd calm me down and let me know everything would be fine. And as soon as the red light came on, I'd walk out and everything clicked. I did a lot of interviews with Vince one-on-one in the ring when he was still commentating ringside.

There was a lot to learn, especially for an old-school wrestler who was about to become a bad guy for the first time. Then there was the issue of becoming this character that was completely at odds with who I am as a person. It was really difficult. I started with Bob Holly on the live-event shows trying to hone my heel skills and develop the character. But for the first six months it just wasn't working well. I was slowly learning how to be a bad guy, but the character wasn't coming out. Vince stayed behind me the whole time. He saw something. He kept talking about the nature of the character. I can't remember who suggested I do something in the ring that had definite sexual overtones. At first I resisted anything like that, but finally, I decided to try something to get the character over. That's when Savio Vega really helped me.

The moment I did something that left no doubt as to Goldust's orientation, the crowd went nuts. It was like turning on a light switch. It was that easy. I locked up with Savio and he said, "Go behind me, take your gold hands, and rub up and down on my chest." I did exactly as Savio directed, then I scampered out of the ring like a coward when he charged me. Everybody went crazy. The fans were screaming, calling me every derogatory name you can think of. It was automatic. I felt it immediately. So I got back in the ring and we locked up again in the corner. Savio said, "Spin me around, turn around, and just shake your butt in my crotch." He pushed me out of the corner and started charging me, and I just ran out of the ring again. They went absolutely ballistic. The response from the audience told me all I needed to know about how to get a reaction. Then running out of the ring got another, larger reaction because the fans were furious that this guy wouldn't get in there and fight Savio fairly.

When it was time for me to whip him, I got on top of him and started rubbing myself, making it look like I was enjoying being on top of this guy. We brought down the house that night, when I figured out how to do the character. I think it actually helped Savio, too, in terms of his popularity. I remember Vince came to one of the shows that followed in Hartford. He said, "I've been hearing some good things about you and Savio, so I'm here to see what all the talk is about." When you make Vince laugh, especially when he's at the curtain with all the other boys, you know you've done something right. That night it was unbelievable when I came through the curtain after the match. The boys were all saying, "You wouldn't believe it. Vince was popping for you. Vince was going crazy over your act." Vince showed that to the other boys, but to me he was more reserved. "Dustin, that was very good. Very entertaining. We're going to take Goldust to the Garden in New York."

Savio and I would draw out the match over twenty to twenty-five minutes and hold the attention of the audience the entire time. We were working hard, but Savio, along with Vince, were the guys who helped get Goldust over.

The suit was extremely hot. I'm used to it now, but it's vinyl and everything on my body is covered. All the pores in my face are covered by the paint, I have gloves, and it is hotter than hell. I used to unzip the suit about halfway down during the match because I was overheating out there. I'd get back behind the curtain and I couldn't get out of the suit fast enough. But as time went on, I was getting in better shape and adjusting to the costume.

Vince followed through and we took the show to Madison Square Garden. Now, Savio is Puerto Rican and there were a lot of Puerto Ricans in the crowd in New York. We were on the undercard, but we took over the place. We gave them the same kind of match that Vince liked in Hartford, and the crowd nearly got out of control. They

were out of their minds. They were so riled up that guys were jumping the rails trying to get to me. The place was sold out and the atmosphere was wild.

The match ended and I walked back through the curtain. I lay down right on the cement floor. I was so hot and exhausted that I could barely breathe. Meanwhile, Savio didn't win, but he was standing in the ring holding up my Intercontinental title belt. Vince leaned over and said, "Man, that was good. You okay?" I told him I was fine, but I needed help to get out of the suit because it was a new one, not completely broken in yet. "Do you feel like going back out there and getting some heat so we can bring this back here next month?" I pulled myself up and said, "Okay."

I didn't know what to do. I ran out there and swung my arm right up between Savio's legs and got him with a shot that knocked him right down. I hit him boom, boom, boom, and left the ring. The fans were beside themselves. I knew Savio wouldn't be upset. He might not have known what exactly was coming, but

With Terri as Marlena.

he knew something was going on and he just went with the flow.

The next month we were the semimain event and we sold out the Garden again. This time we had an even better match. At one point I nearly caused a riot with all those Puerto Ricans in the crowd. I grabbed the microphone and said, "If you Puerto Ricans don't shut up, I'm going to come out there and stick my tongue in each and every one of your throats." They went berserk.

In the beginning, Vince put me with Scott Hall, who was Razor Ramon. Terri was at WWE with me at this point, and although things weren't great between us, life was moving on. But Razor and I didn't click. He didn't like all this suggestive stuff I was doing in the ring. Marlena, which was Terri's character, was like my director. We had an usher boy, Richie, and we'd all sit in director chairs near the ring. I'd be watching Razor wrestle and start rubbing on myself. I sent roses to the ring from Goldust. At one point I walked up to the ring and unzipped my suit while he was beating up his opponent. I stood there licking my lips, then pulled open my suit. I had a big heart painted onto my chest with Razor's name through the middle of it. Razor charged out of the ring after me.

When it came time for us to meet for the Intercontinental Championship on Pay-Per-View, Razor didn't want anything to do with Goldust. Scott and I were on good terms, but he wasn't comfortable with Goldust. He said it was because his kids were at home watching their father on television and he didn't want them seeing another man coming on to their dad that way. Granted, it was a bit much. I didn't really understand or appreciate his perspective at the time because I was just playing a character and doing what I was told. That's when I called Vince and told him I was having issues with Scott.

"You told me to call if I had any problems, Vince. I'm just trying to do the character and he's making it difficult. What should I do?"

Vince told me not to worry about anything. "We're going with you, Dustin. Just keep doing what you're doing." Once in a while Razor would go and talk to Vince, but he'd come out all droopy faced. Vince made it clear he was going with me, and that's all there was to it. For me, that was awesome. Scott had a hard time with it, no question. It all came to a head over in Europe. We were doing our run over there when I hurt my knee in the first minute of one of the first matches. We had to end that match fast because I needed to get to the hospital. We went a couple more days on the tour, but I couldn't work and eventually had to return home. One night we were on a bus heading back to the hotel from one of the shows, and I was drinking

Razor wasn't a big Goldust fan.

a couple beers. Everybody knew Scott's issues. He started getting a little lippy with me. All those guys on the bus were friends: Kevin Nash, Shawn Michaels, and Scott. He just kept running his mouth. I gave it right back at him. As we pulled up to the hotel we were raising our voices. The bus was unloading, but Shawn stayed back as kind of a mediator between Scott and me. We weren't quite to the point where we were going to throw down, but it was pretty intense verbally. We both got to the point where we started crying. We left the bus and we were okay, but it wasn't long after that night that Scott asked for his release from WWE.

He was such a huge star doing all these good things with Kevin, Shawn, and X-Pac. They were like a band of brothers. And here I came in as this outsider doing something that was ahead of its time, on the cutting edge, and working him. Whether his kids were watching or not was irrelevant to me. If he didn't want them watching their father on television, then he should have had the power to make sure they didn't watch. I think it turned out to be just too much for him. I don't know. Maybe he didn't feel he was getting what he expected out of the deal.

Everything was leading up to a match in Miami, where Scott is from. We had come back from Europe and he was chasing my championship. We built up the angle over a couple months and the culmination was supposed to be a Miami Street Fight that would be shown via satellite at *WrestleMania XII* at the Pond in Anaheim, California.

Goldust had arrived and the best part of it all was straight ahead. I'm sure Scott couldn't see what was coming, how awesome it would be. I didn't even recognize what was about to happen.

Facing off against Piper, with a little help from Marlena.

six

THE HARD WAY

My greatest moment in my career started with another phone call from Vince McMahon.

We had just finished taping a television show and I was about to head back home. Razor had left the company a couple weeks earlier and *WrestleMania XII* was a couple weeks away. Vince called and said, "We're flying out to Los Angeles tomorrow morning."

I had no idea what was about to take place. I flew out to Los Angeles with Vince, Bruce Prichard, and Rowdy Roddy Piper. We all got into a limousine and headed to Universal Studios. Along the way, Vince and Bruce explained a concept that would become known as the Backlot Brawl. It sounded awesome. I recognized it was a big step for me personally. Roddy didn't have a problem with Goldust or what we were about to do. He's up for anything.

I had started to take painkillers pretty heavily after my knee injury in Europe. I blew out my left knee, but thankfully I didn't need complete reconstructive surgery. I had an arthroscopic procedure that relieved some of the pain, but after a while I was taking painkillers just to get out of bed in the morning.

One thing my father preached from day one was to avoid drugs. He was adamant about drugs, and for a long time his guidance kept me away from all the illegal ones. On the other hand, painkillers, at least in my mind, were different. I didn't smoke weed. I hated marijuana and I hadn't indulged in cocaine yet. I drank alcohol, but other than some pain pills, that's all I put into my body.

We arrived at the studio and went into a room for a meeting to go over things. Then I went into a dressing room to paint my face and get into my suit. They had some extras screaming our names and an old Cadillac painted gold. I got the old spray-painted Caddy while Roddy got a brand-new white Bronco à la O. J. Simpson.

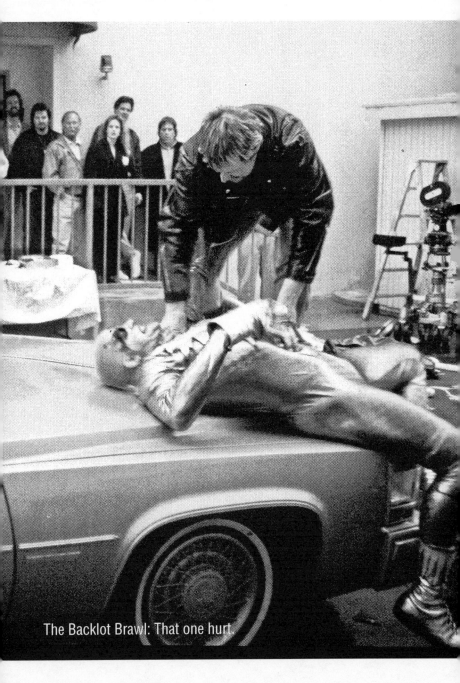

The Backlot Brawl: That one hurt.

After practicing in the cars for a few minutes, we went back into the offices for one last meeting. This was a one-take deal because we were basically going to beat the crap out of one another and demolish pretty much everything in sight, including the cars. The plan was to go right from the cars into a fight. Roddy and I had a pretty good idea of what we wanted to do with all the props. There was a big table with all the catering, a Dumpster, a fire hose, baseball bat, and the cars. There were plenty of things for us to use on our way to the ending. Everything leading up to me driving off with Roddy falling off the hood of the car was pretty much up to us.

The meeting ended and we headed down the lot. I got into my car. The cameras were ready. I was revving the engine just around the corner of the building. The adrenaline was pumping and I was in the zone. It was such a rush because we knew it was a one-shot deal and it was going to be rough. Still, I had no idea what was about to happen. Then, boom, off we went. I took off, cutting the corner squealing the tires, and there was Roddy in between the two soundstages on the back lot with the baseball bat. He was slapping the bat into his hand. I was driving straight toward him and I slammed on the brakes. He threw down the bat and picked up the water cannon. Roddy sprayed the car, then grabbed the bat and smashed the windshield. Then he walked over to my side of the car. The plan was for Roddy to bust out the driver's-side window, so I was ready. I crawled out the other side of the car, and Roddy started beating the crap out of me. He threw me through the table where all the catering and plants were.

All I wanted to do was run into the big steel Dumpster, but Vince didn't want me to display any offense other than one nut shot. Otherwise, Roddy was beating me the whole time. We moved around the car and he clocked me in the head with the bat a couple times, then he threw me into the Dumpster.

Roddy started dragging me along, and that was my shot. *Wham!* I was probably twenty feet in front of the car. I jumped in the car and took off. At that point, Roddy was lying right in the path of the car. He saw me and I could see that he was kind of holding his hand. I could tell his hand was really messed up. The Bronco door was open and I was supposed to clip his car and take the door off. That didn't work out so well. I hit the Bronco but he was still in the way. I was driving pretty slowly because I realized we had one take and I could kill him if I wasn't careful. I was getting closer and closer, and I saw that he wasn't moving. All of a sudden his eyes got bigger and bigger, and we were looking right at one other. It was like everything was happening in slow motion. Then his knees hit the front of my car and he flew right up on top of the car. I was thinking, "I can't stop because we can't shoot this thing again." So I tried to ease my way out of the shot while making sure Roddy was okay.

He looked all right, relatively speaking, of course. I don't know why he didn't get out of the way. I guess Roddy wanted that extra shot of reality. I had only about twenty more feet to go, and I knew he had to roll off the car at some point. As I turned, I ran into that big Dumpster. Roddy finally rolled and I drove away.

One of the real big shots at Universal had his Rolls-Royce parked about fifty yards away, and the Dumpster was rolling straight toward it. The cameraman kept shooting, but at the same time he was running to catch the Dumpster before it crashed into this $300,000 car. Meanwhile, I drove around the corner near the other soundstage and stopped the car. I remember sitting thinking, "What just happened? Holy shit." My suit was ripped, there was blood all over me from Roddy's hand. It was an incredible rush.

We had to duplicate all this two and a half weeks later for *WrestleMania*, so I couldn't wash anything. The whole sequence took about ten minutes, I guess. I could barely walk when I finally got out of the car. I was dizzy as hell, but I wanted to watch it play back on the monitor. All these extras were watching, and I just stood there not saying a word. I walked upstairs and Vince gave us both hugs.

"That was incredible." And it was, but my head was

messed up and so was Roddy's hand. We got back into the limousine and Vince took us to the hospital.

Vince is just one of the boys, and he was on cloud nine as we drove to the hospital. I was on cloud nine, too, but for different reasons. We finally got to the hospital and Roddy went in to get his hand fixed.

We showed up a few days before *WrestleMania*. I had been hanging around Hollywood thinking about what I could do to really take it all to another level, to make the ending of the Backlot Brawl as good as the beginning. I felt like I had to do something to make an impact.

"What can I do that would be outrageous? What can I do to really embarrass myself?" My mind was going as Terri and I walked past Frederick's of Hollywood. Then it hit me. "What if I was wearing women's lingerie with garter belts under my suit? When he beat me up at the end of the match, he could rip off my suit and I'd be standing there with this underwear on. Then you could cover me up and that would be the way it ends?" Terri didn't hesitate. "That would be awesome," she said.

We walked over to the fat girl section at Frederick's and I started trying on lingerie, 10XXX or whatever, to see what we liked. It was just Terri and me, but this is Hollywood, no one raised an eyebrow. I picked out this black outfit and I didn't tell anyone but Vince. He liked the idea, so we were good to go.

Begging for mercy at *WrestleMania XII*.

Kicking Roddy's ass.

When *WrestleMania* rolled around, our cars were parked out behind the arena. As the show went on, the cameras kept going back to Roddy and me riding down a California freeway. The announcer said, "It looks like they're heading this way." Finally we got our cue. We drove down the ramp into the tunnel. I opened my door and Roddy clipped it off with the Bronco. I crawled through the car to the other side and headed into the arena.

Terri was waiting for me, dressed as Marlena. I crawled toward the entrance to the arena. The cameras were there as I crouched down. Then Roddy came walking toward me. We looked exactly the way we had two weeks earlier. We were all beat up, the blood was still on my suit. Marlena was standing there smoking her cigar, and the idea was that I backed myself into the arena not realizing we were at *WrestleMania. Boom!* Roddy's music started blaring. The place went crazy. I was screaming, "No. What am I doing here? I can't believe it, no!" Roddy walked in like he was fixing to stomp me. We made our way to the ring.

At one point, I started kicking him and the crowd was going wild. Roddy reached up and grabbed my crotch, and I yelled, "No, please. Don't. Please don't do that." He bounced me around, then punched me. Bam, I went down. All the crowd wanted was for Roddy to whip me. Boom, boom, boom, and he finally ripped off my uniform, and there was the lingerie. I rolled out of the ring and Terri

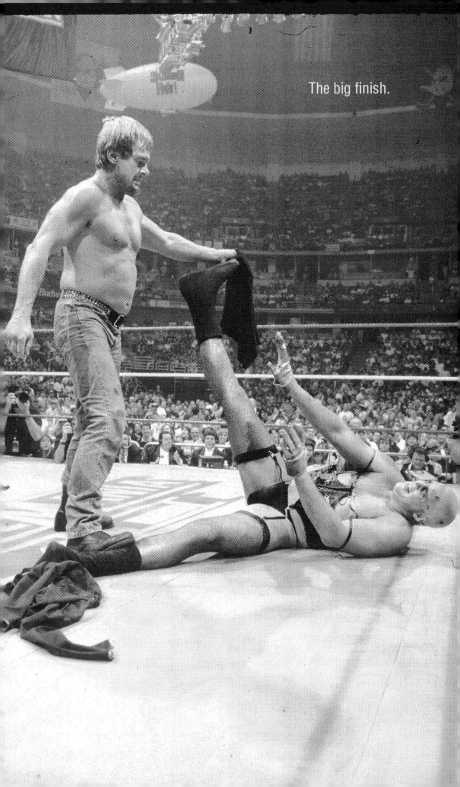

The big finish.

covered me up. We walked to the back and the place went wild. Roddy's son climbed into the ring and they had their moment of glory as the fans erupted. It was unbelievable.

Later that night I gave Roddy's son my Goldust suit.

That was the topper of all toppers right there. Just an incredible experience. Thank you, Roddy.

SEVEN

THE DARKNESS

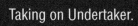
Taking on Undertaker.

Getting booed was awesome, much better than being liked by the fans. Once I figured out how to do Goldust, I knew that if they were booing me, then I was doing something right. It was just so much more fun to get those fans to hate me compared to being a babyface. And it all came together at *WrestleMania XII*.

That event is what finally lifted me out of my father's shadow and dropped me into my own shoes. For the first time I felt like I had an identity of my own that had nothing to do with my father. Shawn Michaels and Brett Hart did their Iron Man Match in the main event, but I was the semimain event and it was truly unbelievable.

I didn't know what my dad thought about the whole Goldust character. In the beginning he probably was embarrassed and really upset about it. That was fine with me. My attitude was, "Bring it on. That's great." I really didn't care. As I've said, I don't know whether Vince got the idea of me playing a character like Goldust because he knew I was estranged from my dad, or he simply thought I was the right guy for the role. These days fans know what side of the bed we sleep on, so who knows? Vince is a very, very creative guy. Maybe he did see the benefit of me playing a character that was 180 degrees from my father, particularly when we weren't talking to one another. Either way, I'm grateful for the opportunity.

Along the way I became okay friends with Shawn Michaels and Hunter (Triple H). Kevin Nash was kind of his own person, but we talked. Other than Razor, I didn't hear a whole lot of talk from the other guys about having a problem with Goldust. Vince was going with me, and if you didn't like it, then you weren't around a whole lot. If I got insecure, or if I felt like things weren't going in the right direction, I'd call Vince and he'd talk me through it. I knew I was doing something right and I trusted Vince.

Despite the success, or maybe because I thought I needed help to keep it all going, I was taking more and more painkillers. I started to get a little sluggish, a little slower in the ring. I complained more, but I had no idea that the drugs had anything to do with my state of mind. There were stressful things going on in my life. My marriage was troubled. I hadn't spoken to my father in a long time, and there was very little reason to think I'd ever speak to him again.

I was physically sore and beat up emotionally. That's not a good combination when you have three hundred or more working days with every one of them in a different city. It seemed reasonable to me that I needed painkillers. Besides, these weren't illegal drugs. Doctors gave them to me. At least that's how I rationalized it all at the time. I just didn't have any idea what was actually happening. I didn't realize the descent was under way, or that the future was about to become a darker shade of gray.

In the months following *WrestleMania*, Goldust was at his height of popularity. My life might have been stressful and difficult outside the ring, but once I walked through that curtain it was magic. After Savio, I had a little bit of an angle with Shawn Michaels. We tore the house down every night because he was the Champion. Suddenly I was wrestling main events everywhere. We were having a great time. I had Goldust down to an art form. I knew exactly when to do something, when to say the perfect line to get the audience on their feet screaming things they didn't even know they were capable of screaming in public. There were guys trying to jump the rail and get into the ring. They threw coins, paper, and all kinds of junk into the ring.

The catchphrase I had developed with Savio came in handy in other places, too. I'd do something to Shawn, then roll out of the ring. Finally, the fans were booing so much that I'd grab the mike and say, "If you don't shut your mouths right now I will come out there and stick my tongue down each and every one of your throats." In New York, they went insane, screaming in Spanish, cussing. So I did that in Detroit with Shawn. This time they started throwing things into the ring. I waved my arms, mouthing to the crowd, "Bring it on," which turned out to be the wrong thing to do in Detroit. I had them so worked up that it almost got out of control. Shawn actually had to leave the ring because there was so much stuff flying in. I just stood there getting pinged with quarters and all the other junk. It was great.

At the end of the run with Shawn, I could see a change in the direction Goldust was heading. Maybe I was becoming a little more insecure, or maybe the drugs were starting to bend my mind.

I did a vignette aimed at Ahmed Johnson, a large African-American superstar. Goldust was naked on a couch. I had my Intercontinental belt lying over me and I was talking all this crazy stuff to Ahmed. Then I pulled out a Hershey's chocolate bar. I start talking about how I just loved the way the chocolate melted in my mouth and stuff like that. It was sick. That led to a shoot we did in Fayetteville, North Carolina. Ahmed was knocked out during a match, and as they pushed him out of the arena on the gurney, I intervened. I pushed the EMS guys back and said, "Oh, I can help him." I started rubbing his head. Then I picked up his face and started giving him mouth-to-mouth, which revived him. When Ahmed woke up, his eyes were wide open like he was freaking out. He got up off the gurney and I took off down the hall. Ahmed was furious, tearing doors off the wall, breaking everything. That led right up to the match where he took my title. Goldust lost the gold to Ahmed Johnson at *King of the Ring* in 1996.

Things were changing. I could feel it. Vince was getting a lot of criticism from different groups. Parents were calling headquarters and complaining about Goldust. Some of them didn't want their kids watching if Goldust was performing. An article in the *New York Times* came out saying gay rights activists were upset over the character. The ratings were good, and as far I was concerned it wasn't my problem. I was having fun doing my job. I couldn't see the larger picture and I'm not even sure how much I cared to see it.

Needless to say, my insecurities started to rise toward the surface. There were a couple times when Vince told me not to do something and I did it anyway. "Don't rub up on anyone in the ring tonight," he said before one match. I did it anyway and he was furious. He told he'd fire me right there on the spot if I ever did something like that again. I apologized, but I still slipped up a couple more times. In a way, I think I knew that it all was coming to an end. The roller coaster was gathering speed on the way down, and I was having a hard time hanging on.

There were highlights, but fewer of them. One of them was a Casket Match with the Undertaker. To this day I'm one of the only guys who ever beat him in a Casket Match. I had Mankind's help that night. We were doing this routine where Mankind was my son and I was his mommy. Sick, no question about it. We built up to the Casket Match and Bruce Prichard wanted to play a joke on Undertaker. The idea was that when I had Undertaker down, and before he sat up, I would crawl between his legs and grab his crotch. It was all in good fun.

At the time, though, I was becoming more and more addicted to Vicodin. The pills helped with my stamina, but the more I took, the more real pain I felt in my body, which was backward.

Slowly the addiction started taking over, though I wasn't conscious of what was happening. Subtle injuries, or aches and pains that I ignore now, led me to take more and more pills. I started drinking more to enhance the effect and cover the pain. I was getting louder in the bars, doing stupid things. Your head can get a little crazy when you suddenly have money and a little bit of power. In my mind, that's all I was doing, no big deal. But looking back I can see how it was becoming a problem.

Once again, life began to imitate art and the walls

started closing in a little, both inside and outside the ring. I worked this angle with Brian Pillman where he kidnapped Terri. Brian had dated her way back before we were married, which of course always made me insecure. I didn't have a problem with him. We were friendly and I did my best to go with the flow, but I was very uncomfortable. I hated that they had a history together. We were working up to a Pay-Per-View, and along the way I was trying to win her back in the matches.

The night before the payoff, we had a live event in Bloomington, Minnesota. We had a pretty good angle going, but Brian was too messed up to work. I don't know what he was taking, but he could barely walk. I remember thinking, "I'm going to have to protect him out there at the same time I've got to protect myself."

We got through the match the best we could. The crowd responded really well and as far as anyone knew, everything was fine. Afterward I walked into the locker room and Brian was sitting in the corner looking like his dog had been shot. I kept asking him if he was okay. Finally, he said, "I don't know, man. I'm just real depressed."

I'd seen that before. There have been guys along the way who took a lot of pills. I'm one of them. I have helped guys to their hotel rooms. I've actually fed them because they were too out of it to put food into their mouths. That's why I never did those kinds of drugs, the downers.

Brian Pillman.

The next morning we flew to St. Louis for the Pay-Per-View. The routine is pretty straightforward: We land, get something to eat, and head to the arena. It was an early call because of the Pay-Per-View, so we were probably scheduled to be at the arena at least five hours before the match. As the day went on, I realized that Brian wasn't at the arena. Finally, I told somebody to call the hotel and check on him. He had looked bad the night before, and I didn't have a good feeling when he wasn't where he was supposed to be, especially for such a big match. Ultimately, they found Brian dead in his hotel room.

It was shocking, but no one had much time to process the horror of it all. The show had to go on and I still had to get out there and perform. It was hard, a lot harder than it looked. All I could do was suck it up and try to tune out reality when that light went on.

A few weeks later, Terri and I did an infamous interview with Jim Ross at the corporate headquarters in Stamford, Connecticut. I was really nervous about the interview. My addiction was making me paranoid. I was drinking more, and things at home were deteriorating quickly. I was never physically violent, but I had become an angry person and verbally abusive to Terri. I thought my anger was justified, but of course it wasn't. None of it was. The drugs and alcohol triggered every one of my insecurities and magnified every slight, whether real or imagined.

In the dressing room prior to the interview, I drank several shots of Crown Royal to calm my nerves. I was ready to unload and I wanted what came out to be real. We talked about my dad and how he was never there when I was younger, or later when I was having problems in my life. I knew they wanted it to go right up the line, but I wanted it to be as powerful as possible. I wasn't drunk, but I was comfortable enough to say anything. The atmosphere was intense because of everything going on in my personal life, particularly with Terri.

Around that time I wanted to wrestle my father on television. Vince never commented one way or another. I didn't actually want to beat my dad, but I thought maybe it would bring closure to our issues. I'm sure Vince thought I'd do something stupid if he gave me the opportunity. It didn't matter, though, because my dad wasn't going to have any part of it. Even after we reconciled, I tried to appeal to my dad's business sense. He wouldn't even consider wrestling me. I always thought Goldust wrestling Dusty Rhodes would have been huge.

The point of the interview with Ross was to get me some sympathy, to make me a good guy. I had burned the Goldust suit on stage with Vince screaming, "Dustin, what are you doing? I gave you this character and you're throwing it away." Everybody went nuts. The interview followed that bit on television where I threw the uniform into the garbage. I remember saying how tired I was of being led around like a little dog. I went off on everybody.

For a while following the interview, I was Dustin Runnels, the artist formerly known as Goldust. But here was my personal life playing out on stage and I didn't see any of it. I didn't see the connection at all because I felt so insecure about everything. If I hadn't been so focused on all the bullshit and so heavy into drinking and painkillers, I would have been where I am right now, only better. Now I can see so clearly how things work, how the business really operates. Back then, I was a mess—and I was the only person who didn't realize it.

After a few weeks as Dustin Runnels, I wanted to do something with Goldust. They weren't doing a whole lot with me at the time, so Vince pulled me up to his office. Terri and Jim Ross were there, too. By then Terri was going off doing her own things as a Diva. Marlena was pretty much done, so she was going in another direction. I had an idea that would get Goldust back into the ring.

"Vince, I want to do something different with this character." I had a person in mind to help Goldust become a crazy, bizarre type of bondage character. I had this picture of being led around on a dog leash with a collar and a ball gag in my mouth. Luna Vachon was the perfect fit for the role. Vince gave the go-ahead and it turned out to be awesome.

Luna was the perfect match for Goldust.

We started with me doing a lot of interviews. Luna would dress me up in these wild outfits. I felt okay about the direction we were going in because I was working again and Vince was giving me the opportunity to get this new version of Goldust over. Vader had been a big star at WCW and I loved working with him there. He was physical as hell, but he knew how to get there. We did all kinds of interviews and they were funny.

One time Nurse Luna was pushing me in a wheelchair, only no one knew it was Luna. Vader said, "Get up out of that chair, punk, because I'm going to whip you." I said, "I can't, Vader, I'm an invalid. You killed me last week. I can't do anything." Vader pushed the wheelchair over, then Luna attacked. I jumped up out of the wheelchair and proceeded to massacre Vader in some goofy outfit. And on we went. It was really bizarre, twisted, sick. In some ways it fit where I was outside the ring. Life was very wacky.

I never had a hard time getting away from it all. When it was time to go to work, I became Goldust. But when the show was over and I pulled on my boots and jeans, I was back to Dustin. But the once-normal Dustin now was far from normal. He was getting rowdy, drinking too much, and taking too many pills. I was getting worse, but I still couldn't see it. And really, I didn't care. I'd go home and get into arguments with Terri. She saw how many pills I was taking. She knew—it would have been obvious to anyone close to me.

Vince Russo has quite the imagination and he helped me a lot. I had a very positive experience with him. All those interviews I did with movie references and the sexual double entendres, every one of them came out of his sick mind. I never had a problem with Vince, though. When they weren't pushing me, I became mad at everybody. It's incredible, but I didn't realize that I was the problem. That's what drugs do to you. You don't know what you're doing to yourself because you can't see clearly. I became more paranoid and insecure about everything. The abuse was tearing a hole in my life.

I was on the road with Terri for some of the live events. I was working, doing fine, but I was getting lower and lower on the card. I was losing more often, which in and of itself wasn't necessarily a big deal. When I had the Intercontinental Championship I lost a lot, but I had more heat than anybody else. This time, it felt different. I'm not sure that it actually was different, but it didn't feel the same. We were on our way to Birmingham, Alabama, driving down from Nashville. I was pilled up and I called the office.

"Guys, I'm hurting, man, I don't want to go tonight."

They let me have it. "Dustin, you get your ass there. Do your job. We'll talk about this later, but get your ass there and do your job tonight."

I ended up going, but shortly thereafter I quit. Life was just bad. Terri and I decided we needed to move back home to Live Oak, Florida, where she is from. We talked about building a house there. Terri kept working, and I figured I could find enough work to make ends meet. I figured maybe I'd do something for WCW, but in reality I was burned out and exhausted. The pills were taking a terrible toll on me physically, mentally, and emotionally. I was beat up, depressed, and falling apart. I still hadn't spoken to my father.

Everything just seemed to be getting . . . darker.

Things got a little freaky.

EIGHT

THE FALSE BOTTOM

Dakota was five years old when we moved back to Florida and into my mother-in-law's house.

Over the next few months, about all I did was hang out around the house drinking and strategizing my next pill run. By then I was constantly medicated, pretty much every waking hour. Terri wasn't stupid. She knew. I was becoming angrier and more messed up with each passing day. Finally, she brought me into the bedroom one afternoon.

"Dustin, we're getting a divorce."

I never saw it coming, which goes to show how removed I was from reality. To me it was completely out of left field. We talked about it a little bit, then she brought Dakota into the room so we could tell her together. Dakota started crying. She didn't understand why her mommy and daddy were no longer going to be living with her. I was trying to hold it together, but I couldn't. I broke down, and that ticked off

Terri even more because she didn't want Dakota to see me crying. Meanwhile, all I could think about was what Terri was doing to me. I was so self-absorbed and screwed up that I couldn't see past my own pain, all of which I had created. I started apologizing, pleading with Terri to give me another chance. But she was done and I was destroyed.

A few weeks later I needed to find a place to live. I didn't care where I ended up, but I had to leave that house. In the middle of everything, I decided to give Eric Bischoff a call. I have no idea why I thought that was a good idea. Yet it turned out to be a great idea. Eric knew I had been fired by the WCW. He also knew I took it like a man and never pushed the issue legally. To his credit, Eric didn't forget.

I went up to Atlanta and he gave me a great deal for really decent money. I went back to Florida, found a Realtor, and bought the second house I saw. I tried to convince myself that I had accepted the reality of the divorce and that my life was going to change. The fact that I had a great contract no doubt helped me deal with those issues, but my feelings about the divorce were still raw. I started buying everything. After the house, I bought a truck and a boat. In my twisted mind I was going to show Terri that everything was actually her fault. All I could see was what was happening to me. She had kicked me out. She had taken me from my daughter. I couldn't see even a little bit of myself in the middle of it all, and yet the whole thing started and ended with me.

It wasn't her fault. She loved me. She took care of me. I chose the wrong path and the marriage didn't last. Fortunately, a beautiful and wonderful daughter came out of our time together. Now everything is good between Terri and me, but I was so messed then that I had no idea how much more messed I would become.

That period was probably my first bottom, but it was a false bottom. I had a whole lot farther to fall before it all ended. But I dug myself out financially and went through the divorce. I had Dakota every other week. I was working at WCW, making huge support payments, and working hard to function when my daughter was around. I was still popping pain pills left and right, but the alcohol consumption hadn't picked up yet. I was drinking, just not as much as I did later.

As I've said, the pills had an uplifting effect on me. They made me feel more energetic and raised my mood. I'd take a couple pills before an interview, and I could talk forever. It just flowed out of me. I'd start spitting out stuff and it all made perfect sense to me.

One day I heard that Barry Windham was doing a shoot up at his property near Homerville, Florida, just outside Jacksonville. I'm about four-wheeling, hunting, fishing, and everything that goes along with that lifestyle. I loved seeing the camera crew work and having fun with guys I really liked, so I drove over from High Springs.

Before the shoot we went to the Jacksonville Coliseum, where there was a show that night. Barry told me, "You know, your dad is in the building."

Somebody had gone inside and told my father that his son was outside in the parking lot. When I realized he knew I was there, it felt like time stopped. I was scared because I didn't know what would happen. I didn't know whether my father was about to come out of the building and punch me, or reach out and shake my hand. I was standing in the parking lot with Barry and Curt Hennig watching the door when it slowly opened.

I hadn't seen my father in the flesh in five years. He started walking toward me. The cowboy hat kind of hid his face and he was walking in his unmistakable strut. It took him forever to get to me. Meanwhile, everyone got real quiet. I couldn't see his eyes. I was trying to figure out what was about to happen, but I couldn't get a read. He finally came within a couple feet of me and he lunged toward me. He hugged me and we stood there squeezing one another for probably twenty minutes. It was so emotional. Five years of heartache and pain came falling out of both of us. It was like being reborn.

For me, it was an immediate feeling of becoming lighter, as if a tremendous weight had been lifted off my back. From that point on we never turned back. It's like we finally grew up. We knew that after that experience we had to think about what words we chose to use. If there was something he wanted to get across to me, he thought about what he wanted to say. I learned that I too had to think about how I expressed myself. He's my dad. I realized that he could be gone any day. We became closer than we had ever been, closer in a way that I had craved and needed when I was little.

I learned that if you are a parent and you don't understand your children, then you need to tell them, "Hey, you've got one mom and one dad in life. Don't let that relationship slip by you. Once they are gone, they are gone forever. Don't wait and hope for a second chance that might never come." If you are a parent and you never tell your kids that you love them, then they are going to grow up craving that attention. They'll eventually find it somewhere else. If you can get them now before issues come between you, then you are going to be much better off. By being honest and open with your feelings, everyone involved gains a better understanding of the other person. You create a platform and an atmosphere that allow your relationship to grow even through differences of opinion. Make sure your children know how much you love them. If you are the son or daughter, try to understand where your parent is coming from before it's too late.

I will say this: If you are a parent and your son or daughter is communicating with you, then you are doing something right. It's that simple. If your child comes to you for advice or guidance without you asking if everything is okay, then you are doing something right. That shows everyone is on the same page. It shows mutual respect, happiness, love, and trust.

Once Dad and I got back together, he was very supportive. It was like those five years never happened. He was there when the divorce went through. And there was a good feeling between us, better than it had ever been previously.

The character Seven was a result of our getting back in touch. One day we were at my dad's place in Atlanta. My brother, Cody, was there. I wanted to discuss with them a new character I had been thinking about. I mentioned the name Seven, then described how he looked, how he acted, the way he talked, just everything about him. We came up with the actual vignettes right there at my dad's place. Cody and I even shot a little scene that turned into the character. Really, I looked like Uncle Fester with red eyes, white face paint, and a shaved head. I thought it was really cool when Seven would come up to the window of his house as this scary, dark guy talking in a real low voice with a kind of demonic element to him.

In the scene we shot at my dad's house, I came up out of the bushes to the window. It was creepy but cool. I showed it to Eric back at the office and he got us a budget. We had enough money for a couple extras to shoot some really freaky vignettes.

I was wearing a very thick, long leather coat that I had designed. It probably weighed fifty pounds. The coat was very elaborate—it looked like Pinhead's coat in the *Hellraiser* movies. We spent $20,000 setting all this up and everything appeared to be fine and ready to go when Vince Russo showed up. He had other ideas.

"What do you think about going out there and just cutting a promo as Dustin, not this Seven character?"

Russo left it up to me, but he made a persuasive argument and I just went with it. Seven—one night only! I don't know, I think it would have been pretty good. Russo mentioned something about the character being too dark, too creepy for kids. We did one vignette with a small kid. The character was wearing the long dark coat and looking into the child's bedroom. You heard Seven say, "Now close your eyes and go to sleep, my child." When the kid opened his eyes, they were black. Apparently, they thought that was a bit too much. At least that was one of the excuses for killing off the character, which was ridiculous and stupid. Think of some of the other things you've seen on television. I know it was kind of creepy, but the vignettes were cool.

I designed pretty much every aspect of the character, the vignettes, everything. But Russo was the boss, the head dude. He gave me creative freedom to an extent. I'm sure that if I had told him I wanted to keep doing Seven, Russo would have put an X on the whole thing. In a lot of ways I was still blind to the gritty part of my job.

Russo wanted me to go out there as Dustin and cut a promo about how my dad was unfairly fired by WCW. Russo wanted me to go off on him, too, for dressing me up and making me do all these gimmicks. The idea was that I was tired of all the interference, and that I was Dustin Rhodes, dammit, and I was going back to my roots.

When I landed in the ring I took the microphone and I went off. I went off on Vince Russo, Vince McMahon, and everybody, including the WCW for kicking my dad to the curb. We were in Atlanta and the fans went nuts.

It was a good promo, but I think Russo was just trying to get some heat for himself. Nothing really happened after that. I wore the coat into the ring, but the paint was gone and I was Dustin, the American Nightmare. Eventually, I was just put on the shelf. I was making good money, but I wasn't getting any kind of push. They weren't doing anything with me. I don't know if Russo was the one behind it all. I wrestled occasionally, then headed home and collected paychecks. But that's the story of Seven—created and killed off in one night.

I did a little run with Jeff Jarrett, who was a very close friend of Russo's. I guess that was Russo's way of helping out his buddy, because I lost all the time. Of course I knew it wasn't about winning and losing, but it just didn't feel right at the time. There wasn't much reason for me to be losing, or winning, for that matter, because we weren't building a story line. I felt lousy and I had too much time to think about it.

I started wondering why Russo would be messing with me. I couldn't understand what was happening to me, and I wasn't sure what was happening to the business either. I knew there were guys who hated my dad, but I was Dustin, not Dusty. So they hated me, too? I never did anything to those people.

Looking back, though, I realize that Vince doesn't do anything that doesn't make sense. If he doesn't believe you're going to make him money, then he won't use you. It's that simple. But back then I didn't know what was going on. All I knew is that I wasn't working a whole lot. Too much free time combined with the growing list of issues with Terri was a good recipe for disaster.

The truth is, I was a mess. Terri is a really good woman, but I put her through so many bad experiences and it was all coming back to bite me. I blamed her for all the pain I felt around the divorce and the fact I could see my daughter only every other week. Eventually that pain turned into hate, which is far more toxic for the person feeling that emotion.

There wasn't much room for my angels. My demons were taking control.

nine

THE DESCENT

When I left the WCW I didn't do much of anything for a while. I did some shows for independents, but mostly I was chasing pain-killers and living off what I made on my last contract. That is, until I blew it all.

It wasn't just the money. I was taking more and more pills. I also had a short-lived and highly volatile second marriage. We only dated for a few months, then one day we just went to the justice of the peace and did the deed. That was typical of the way my mind was working—wasn't working is probably a better way to describe it.

It started during my final weeks at WCW. We were married only a year. There was just so much going on at the time. There were child support issues with Terri. I was worried about my house being taken away from me. Cars were repossessed. My life was spinning out of control and generally chaotic. I was starting to sell everything I had just to buy my next bottle of pills. I spent a lot of time every day thinking. "Okay, which doctor am I going to go to when my pills run out?" I always had two or three doctors. Days in advance of running out, I'd be planning, trying to figure out which one I could call to get the next bottle.

It took a lot of time, focus, and effort to manage that part of my life. As a result, time was taken away from Dakota. Of course I didn't see it that way. I would wake up thinking and planning. "Okay, I'm going to pick me up a bottle of vodka before I get my pills, then I'll be good. I'll be fine." That process might take five minutes on a good day, ten hours on a bad day. I was at the point where I needed that fix to feel better before I could think or do anything else. As bizarre as it sounds now, I honestly didn't think anyone was the wiser. I couldn't imagine the possibility that people around me knew I was hiding bottles of pills or spiking Mountain Dew with a pint of vodka. I had a prescription. I wasn't doing anything illegal. Well, that part isn't necessarily true. Let's just say I wasn't doing any illegal drugs.

I had beer around the house and legal drugs. No big deal. Over time, though, the drinking went to a whole new level. Still, I thought I was hiding everything from everyone. But I was taking so many pills. By that point I was up to twenty painkillers a day, then three to five Xanax at night so I could sleep.

Here's a story that still scares me. I ran out of Xanax one night. I knew I couldn't get any more for three days. On the third night without the pills, I started experiencing horrific withdrawals. I was lying in bed, completely beat up and exhausted, but I couldn't get to sleep. I didn't know what time of day it was, whether the sun was coming up or just about to go down. There were times during the day when I tried to sleep because I thought it was nighttime.

The next morning at around six o'clock, I called Terri to wish Dakota "Sweet dreams" before she went to bed. She had just gotten up and was getting ready for school and I didn't have a clue. Thank God it wasn't my week with Dakota. After I hung up, I somehow realized how messed up I was. I called Terri and came up with this story about how I had been on the road and I was just real tired.

Meanwhile, I was working independents and trying to hold it all together. I'd take a couple pain pills to get me through the match, then head home as soon as I could get out of the arena. There isn't much money in the independent game. A guy had to stay busy to make any kind of living. I didn't care about making a living. All I cared about was making enough cash to buy my pills, a gallon of vodka, and gas for my truck.

I did some shows as Goldust, which was illegal because WWE owned the intellectual property. If WWE had ever known, they would have sued me to block the use.

I just didn't care. Besides, I could make $1,500 a night as Goldust. It was an easy decision. Then again, my decision-making process was rather limited. A lot of times I'd decide whether to do a show based on the venue's proximity to my house. I avoided getting on planes. I'd work Florida, if it was close enough, and I'd consider the Carolinas if the money was right. Keep in mind most of the time I was getting paid $500, $800, or maybe $1,000, but it was sporadic. I always demanded cash, never checks. I had seen my father get screwed over taking checks that didn't clear. If it was convenient and easy, then I'd try to sell some pictures in the arena. Most of the time, though, I just wanted to do my work and get out of town.

Physically, I was a mess. I was out of shape and getting fat. Looking back, it's amazing I didn't have a serious injury during that period. I made sure to keep what I had to do in the ring to a minimum. If I was Dustin Rhodes, then I did some Goldust moves and let the other guy beat me up a little bit, though not to the point of injury. Believe me, that's a lot harder than it looks, especially in the shape I was in.

When I went up to visit my dad in Atlanta, I'd have bottles of pills and bottles of vodka hidden in my bag. I had everything right where I could find it at all times. He didn't know that I was pouring vodka into Mountain Dew bottles, or stopping back in the bedroom where I was sleeping in to fill the bottle back up with vodka. I didn't realize that when you drink that much alcohol, it starts coming out of your pores and you smell like a distillery. That's one of the many signs of a serious problem, hiding your behavior from people and believing you are doing it successfully. My dad had been around the block and he knew what addiction looked like. But I don't think he had any idea about how much I was doing and where it was headed.

In the middle of all this, I made another horrible choice for a girlfriend. Basically she was just a really bad lady. That's when I started adding cocaine to the mixture. We were both highly dysfunctional, but she took it all to a whole new level. Of course, that didn't stop me from having her take care of Dakota when I was away.

Eventually, and thanks to my dad, I started working for Total Nonstop Action for $1,000 a show. He was the boss, right under Dixie Carter. TNA wasn't doing too well at that point, but I had a job making okay money. I could drive home just about every night. All I was doing was what little I had to do in the ring, then hanging out spending my money on coke, pills, and booze.

I started making excuses for why I couldn't spend time with Dakota. Subconsciously I probably knew I didn't want her around me or my girlfriend because the environment was so toxic. Despite the chaos, I showed up every night for work. I have no idea how I was able to stay on point with work at that time. One of my cardinal rules was never to drink before I worked a match. I wouldn't consider doing coke before a match either. I'd take painkillers, fine. I had been taking painkillers for so long that I had convinced myself I really needed them. I was taking medicine because I worked in a tough business. That was the story I had cemented into my mind. But drugs have a way of altering everything, including the stories you tell yourself. Eventually I started doing a little coke before matches while retaining my vow to never drink alcohol before I got into the ring, as if that was something to be proud of.

The next bottom was right around the corner. We did a Pay-Per-View event, and I had a really good match that night. My girlfriend was in our suite with my daughter at the Hard Rock Hotel in Orlando. I went back to the room feeling really good about my performance. I had a couple drinks to kind of settle down. Meanwhile, I realized she had been drinking all day long. She drank a giant bottle of Jack Daniel's, all of it. She was a mess, starting to get loud and crazy. I was in the other room trying to get Dakota to sleep. I kept telling this woman to keep it down. I should have known what was coming next.

She lost it. She started screaming and telling me that she was going to go sleep with Dakota. By then I had had more than enough. I said, "I can't do this anymore. Get out right now." As I was getting her things together and stuffing them into a bag, she continued screaming. I dragged her out of the bedroom where I had been trying to get Dakota to sleep and put her bags outside the door. She was fighting to prevent me from throwing her out of the room. As soon as I got the door open, I eased her out and that was it. Or at least that was it until the police arrived. My daughter was in the other room as I was trying to explain what happened. I never hit the woman or did anything at all violent. All I did was ease her out of the room. They didn't want to hear a word I had to say. It turned out that she had multiple drugs and alcohol in her body, things I didn't even know about. She was completely out of control.

Terri's response was reasonable, and horrible. She wouldn't let me see Dakota alone. I attended anger management classes. I spent three days in jail. It was awful, but I went through all of it. When I got out of jail, my dad was there. He gave me a hug and told me to get my life straight.

Over time, Terri started slowly letting me back into Dakota's life, but I couldn't see her alone for a long time. Initially, our only time together took place at a visitation center. I knew the people there were trying to protect the children. I understood they were doing their jobs, but I hated it. The center was a house with a backyard. There were things to do with your child, but there was some-body watching you every minute. Dakota was a smart little kid. I'm sure her mother told her what was going to hap-pen, but Dakota just wanted her dad. I thought I had my

My dad could work the crowd like none other.

demons under control, but I didn't have *anything* under control. All I knew was that her mother kept taking me to court. To me, she was making my life more miserable than it already was by keeping my daughter away from me. I knew Dakota wanted everything back to the way it used to be when she could spend an entire week with me. There were plenty of times when I was crying. In a lot of ways, that was the beginning of the end.

I still needed to work, and Steve Corino, an independent, was part of the management for Zero-One wrestling, which combined with the Pride Fighting Championship in Japan. He put together a run in Japan for my dad and me as a tag team. It was good money and I was able to be with my father. It was an easy decision for me. My dad still had that incredible charisma. All he had to do was raise an elbow and the crowd, no matter where in the world he went, would go crazy.

He was almost sixty years old at the time and I was in my late thirties. I couldn't help myself by then. I was messed up one night in Japan, too. I still didn't think my dad knew what I was doing, but looking back I'm not sure how he couldn't have known. I was drinking heavily pretty much throughout the day, every day. It was the first time I had drinks before I worked, and it showed in the ring. A couple minutes into the match I actually thought I was having a heart attack: I couldn't breathe, I was sweating.

Those boys over there go hard and fast, and it's very physical. There was my dad, who had been doing this for forty years and probably had more aches and pains than I can imagine, and he was doing every bit as much work as I was. But I was ready to collapse. I felt like I was dying. There were probably seventy thousand people in the arena and it was the last night, the big show. I had been scheduled to go on the next trip to Japan, too, but they didn't bring me back.

†EΠ

THE RAIN ON THE HILL

I don't remember how I ended up back at WWE, but I signed a two-year contract in 2002. Another chance at a time when I couldn't believe I had any left. It was either my fifth or sixth go-round with WWE, which had bought the WCW prior to my return.

I went back as Goldust, only this time he was more comedic than dark. One of the bits we did was Goldust getting electrocuted. As a result of the shock he developed Tourette's syndrome. I guess since Tourette's isn't life-threatening they figured it was okay to laugh at someone with the problem. Batista and Randy Orton threw me into an electrical panel and I suddenly started speaking in this halting, stuttering kind of a way. I'd start to say something that sounded as if I was going to say a curse word or something terribly off-color. I'd draw out the consonants, stuttering and trying to spit out the word. Finally, when I got

Booker wasn't feeling the love.

the word or sentence out of my mouth it was something else entirely, which of course was part of the joke.

That's also when Booker T and I came together as sort of the odd couple. It was supposed to be a one-shot deal, but we had real chemistry together. In one episode, we did a scene called "A Night at the Movies" as sort of Siskel and Ebert characters. We talked about *The Scorpion King*, the Rock's first big movie, and everyone loved how that came out. So they put us together and we continued to do all kinds of spoofs. We did some cool stuff. Booker is a real good guy and we had a lot of fun. People were popping for us like crazy. At the time, Booker T was thinking about joining the nWo, which was hot. One of the spoofs had me showing up everywhere, just shadowing Booker T. I'd show up in a different costume every time. I was still Goldust, but we'd add something to make me look like Undercover Brother, Darth Vader, the Crocodile Hunter, crazy stuff. I'd try to talk him out of joining the nWo so he could join forces with Goldust. "Come on, Booker T. Together with Goldust we'll become the Tag-Team Champions of the world."

We ran that story for weeks and it was really working. Finally we started tagging together and it just clicked. One day, we shut down a 7-Eleven for a shoot. I was dressed up like the basketball player Latrell Sprewell. I had my gold paint, but I also had a basketball jersey and gold chains around my neck. Booker was walking through the store talking about how he had to get his prematch Slurpee. Meanwhile, I was sneaking around the store.

"You didn't see no gold freak in here, did you?" Booker asked.

Just then I walked up to him talking in Goldust's voice.

Finally he said, "What are you doing here, man?"

I was eating a hot dog and I said something like, "If you let me be your partner, Booker, I'll let you take a bite out of my weenie." People just loved it. From that point, fans knew that every week they would see Goldust stalking Booker and that it would be funny as hell.

I was getting a big push and the combination of Booker and me was working. Then right in the middle of it all, they took Booker away from me. We had become Tag-Team Champions, but they wanted to push Booker in singles. That's fine in retrospect. At the time I didn't understand why they would kill something that was working so well. I don't know whether Booker was tired of the whole thing, or whether our bit had run its course.

I bounced around for four or five years. I did the bit at TNA and shuttled between independents when I wasn't completely absorbed by finding my next bottle of vodka or pills.

At TNA, Vince Russo and I came up with the Black Reign character. I was working as Dustin Rhodes, but I wasn't working that often, so we came up with the idea that Dustin had this split personality, BlackReign. It wasn't much of a stretch given my life at the time. Russo said, "Just flip out and go nuts." One night during an interview with one of the announcers, that's exactly what I did. I started out talking really calmly, then I went crazy. That was the birth of my alter ego, Black Reign.

The character was pretty dark, which fit the color of my personal life. He came out with black and silver face paint that I did myself. Black Reign also carried around a huge pet rat that I had to travel with. I went through three rats, and a couple of them were mean as could be. One of the bits involved me putting the rat into a pillowcase. I'd grab my opponent and open the pillowcase over his head so it looked like the rat was biting his eyes out or tearing his face apart. Then I added an accessory. I started carrying a weapon that my girlfriend, Ta-rel, found at a Renaissance fair. It was a real old-world war hammer with a big spike on the end. It was a dangerous weapon. So I had that in one hand and the rat in the other. I'd hit guys in the head with the hammer, or put the rat on them.

Russo came up with the rat idea, which tells you a little bit about how his sick mind works. I was scared of the damn thing at first. It took me a while to get used to the rats because every one of them was huge. With TNA we weren't traveling in airplanes very often, so I had to cage the rat at home. I kept the rat locked up, then loaded the cage into the car and drove to a match. The original rat died. The second one was Misty No. 2, a big white rat. It was so nasty that I had to wear welding gloves to pull it out of the cage. It tried to bite me every time I went to grab it. One day I had to do an interview with another wrestler. I had the welding gloves on, but the rat didn't want any part of coming out and sitting through an interview. We decided to send out a runner to find a new, and hopefully more cooperative, rat. Meanwhile, I put the cage, with the rat inside, into my car and went back inside to prepare for the interview. After about three hours I realized, "Oh, no, the rat's in the car." I ran outside and it was fried, stiff as a board. I thought I had kept the windows down in my little Honda Civic, but apparently not. It must have been 120 degrees in the car, and the rat was gone. Thankfully, they found another rat and the show went on. We called the third one Misty as well, but the rat was a male, so his name became Mr. Mister. He was awesome. I'd let him out of the cage at home and he'd crawl up on the couch and go to sleep. I had a cat and a dog and neither one bothered Mr. Mister. It was like having a third pet.

That last little bit of time was the hardest period of my life. It's remarkable I lived through it because I was riding a rocket toward the bottom.

Every morning, as soon as I pulled myself out of bed,

I'd take three Vicodins or Lortabs just to get moving. I was sore and pretty banged up physically, but over time pain pills exaggerated rather than eliminated whatever pain I was feeling. It was a slow process for me to get into the day. I'd get that first rush from the pills and then I'd get moving. I might do something around the house, or jump into my truck and drive to the river to work on this book.

I wrote probably fifty pages longhand sitting in my truck out near the river in High Springs. I'd just sit there drinking and writing. I wrote some bitter stuff. I recognized I had a problem, though I didn't understand the true nature of what was happening. I didn't have any idea about how to get help for myself, but there I was dispensing wisdom to the masses. The irony of course is that I used that process to deal with my own problems. I knew I was a mess. My rationale was to write a book that would warn, then help others who might be temped to drive down the dead-end road I was living on. I didn't have the coping skills or the tools to deal with my own problems, though.

I wanted to quit taking all the pills. I was conscious of the need to do so, but I was horrified by the prospect of going through withdrawal and having all those demons back in my dreams. I'd tell myself, "Okay, today is the day. I'm going to quit." For a couple days I'd slow down, cut back on the amount I was taking. Then it would all pick up again. I went down to the river just about every day. I'd prop my feet up, turn on the radio, drink, and write. After a couple hours I'd go home. I might take a nap, but when I woke up I'd take some more pills and head to the bar with a buddy. That was my life.

The horrible thing about drugs, particularly painkillers, is that the more you take the more you hurt. That's how it starts. If I was taking ten a day, I thought I needed to take fifteen. Once fifteen pills didn't kill the pain, then I took twenty or twenty-five.

There were several times when I thought I couldn't do it anymore. At one point I was taking money from my mother and father to pay bills. Instead of actually paying the bills, I'd buy another bottle of booze or some more pills. Eventually my living conditions started to deteriorate. I went from one trailer park to another. At the end I was living in a one-room "apartment" attached to a house. It had been a garage that the owner enclosed. He put in a kitchen and bathroom for me, but it was tiny. I had my dog and a roof over my head. Beyond that, all I cared about were the drugs and alcohol.

I was working independents here and there, getting deeper and deeper into the addiction. Then I came across an angel, the woman I have been with for the last six years.

It was as if Ta-rel was dropped out of heaven to save my sorry self at a time when I wouldn't have blamed anyone for kicking me to the curb and never looking back.

For the most part, she took care of me when I couldn't take care of myself or didn't care enough to take care of myself. She kept me living long enough that I could be saved. I have long promised myself never to get married again, but if I ever do, it will be to her. She doesn't drink, but she was a bartender at a place in High Springs where I hung out and got drunk. It's amazing I had the presence of mind even to acknowledge her. I didn't give a damn about anyone or anything at the point she entered my life. She saw me at my absolute worst and for some reason never left my side.

For about the last month leading up to the end I was living in this little box. Ta-rel, my angel, would come over and visit me. We would sit up and watch movies, maybe share some food. All the while I'd be drinking. I also have attention deficit disorder, so I always had to be doing something else, too. Usually, it was something creative. I have always been artistic. I have designed logos, T-shirts. Even during my descent into hell, when times were tough with Terri and I didn't have Dakota after my arrest, I spent all day and night drinking and making very intricate wooden crosses. Each one had a different tribal design with paint and designs. I created necklaces with really cool stainless-steel beads I picked up at a store near my house. I had all the necessary tools. I've always liked doing things with my hands. I made crosses for my father and sister.

That's why I could sit by the river and write. I have always loved to draw and create. So I'd sit there with my dog, drinking and drawing. I was taking pills, drinking vodka with Mountain Dew, and eating those cheap little frozen party pizzas. That's it. That was my life.

I became so fearful of not being able to fall asleep that I was up to fourteen to twenty milligrams of Xanax. There were times when I fell asleep with food literally hanging out of my mouth. Then I'd wake up and not even realize I had been to sleep. So I'd pop a few more Xanax. By the time the night was over, I had taken enough pills to knock over a horse. It's incredible what the human body can withstand and the level of drug tolerance you can build up. I was probably taking close to forty pills a day at the end. I was so desperate that I actually bought pain pills from drug dealers because I would run out long before I could find another doctor to write a prescription. If I dropped a pill and it fell into the carpet, I would spend hours down on my hands and knees trying to find it. At the same time I was drinking so much that I'd wake up dizzy and unable to walk.

Finally, after a three-day binge, I'd had enough. It was

raining. I pulled myself up and walked right out the door. The rain was pouring down and I stumbled up a hill near this house where I knew I could get cell-phone reception. Somehow I managed to call my dad. It was four thirty in the morning. I was falling down the hill in the mud. Ta-rel was trying to hold me up. I scared my dad half to death. I managed to get back into the house, soaking wet.

I had found the bottom.

As soon as I woke up, I called Ann Russo, who works for talent relations at WWE. She handles everything in the office and truly saved my life.

Ann took care of everything. One of the wonderful things about WWE is that it will take care of anyone who has a problem. If you have ever been a part of the WWE family, they don't turn their back on you.

On the way to rehab everyone kept calling to make sure I was actually getting on the plane. I had every intention of getting on the plane, but I also had every intention of getting blasted one last time. I was in Delta's Crown Room drinking as much as I could and taking every pill I could get my hands on.

It took me eight days to detox. The first four days I slept. The last four days were unbelievably bad. I don't ever want to go back again. I spent thirty days locked away facing my demons and trying to stare down all of them. Every emotion comes spilling out, but the dominant one is fear. Once you break through the physical addiction and start to realize what you have done and what you have to do to remain sober, it's incredibly scary. Some of the other people in there with me said they were afraid ever to go outside again. For the first time in years for some of us, we felt good.

ELEVEN

THE ESCAPE

It took a couple weeks in rehab before the pain began to subside and the fog slowly started to lift. I was still shaky and far from clearheaded, but around the two-week mark I started to think about what I would see when I walked back out into the world. It had been so long since I looked at anything without one vice or another coursing through my body that the thought of leaving was scary.

It's hard for someone who hasn't gone through it to understand, but without all those crutches stuffed into all those bottles, the world seems like a dangerous place. Before long, everyone in rehab is thinking the same thing: I don't want to leave this place because I'm safe in here.

By the time day thirty rolled around, I was extremely nervous. My counselor suggested I stay another sixty days, but I felt like I could make it out here on my own with support groups and my sponsor. Thankfully, I wasn't alone.

I had my angel, Ta-rel, by my side every step of the way. But it was strange when I started to see the world through the eyes of a newborn. For the first time in a long time, I saw the world as it really was rather than how it appeared with drugs and alcohol running through my system. I had done so much of both over the previous ten years that my body wasn't close to being back to normal, even after thirty days.

I was in one of the best facilities in the world, but there is very little joy in rehab. I was in with people who had problems at least as bad as mine, some of them a lot worse. Then there were a couple people who had been caught drinking and driving and had been ordered into rehab by a judge. They hated being there and did everything in their power to make the experience as miserable as possible for everyone else. There were a couple guys who wanted to fight. And everyone, at one point or another, hated his or her counselors. At the very least, I had to learn how to take suggestions.

Now instead of fighting my feelings, I accept having a bad day. Everyone has them. I don't put as much pressure on myself anymore. I acknowledge the fact I'm having a bad day, and then I move on. I begin and end every day with a prayer. All I know is that the process has worked for me. I've been given the tools and I now understand how to use them. I also see that life gets better when you apply those tools. I know what relapse means and I have no interest in experiencing the options relapse presents— jail, another stint in an institution, death. At the same time, I don't look into the future. For me it's one day at a time. I think it will be that way for the rest of my life. All I can handle is what's happening right now in front of me. I don't worry about things beyond my control. If I'm going to work with Ezekiel Jackson tonight, I know that he's going to slam me down in the ring and there're going to be lightning bolts of pain shooting down my body. Can I do anything about that? No. I can ask him to knock me down a little softer, but that's about all. That's a lot different from worrying about it and being unable to say a word because of some insecurity. I've learned to communicate, which in turn has helped me improve my life. If I have a question, I go right to the source and ask. That's a big change for me.

It isn't simply a matter of learning new tools to deal with life. You have to be ready and willing to change. Every second of every minute of every day requires a certain level of focus. It's intense, to say the least. But I was willing to look at the areas of my life that had suffered because of my addiction. It's not pretty and it's not easy, but it's absolutely necessary if you hope to recover. It is, and always will be, a one-day-at-a-time process for me.

A lot of people either aren't prepared for that process,

or they haven't reached bottom where they are willing to put themselves through that kind of examination. Then there are others who never learn no matter how many times they go through a program. I know the numbers. I know that the vast majority of people relapse. But I also know I'm not going to be one of them. I passed two years clean and sober on May 20, 2010, and I have no intention of ever going back to the life I was living before I got help.

I'm on the right path. I'm doing my program day by day. But those demons are always on my shoulder. At any given time I could turn around and start listening to them whispering in my ear. I could choose that bad path again, or I could find a support program to keep those demons at bay. Does it scare me? Hell, yes. There's alcohol and drugs everywhere in our society. All you have to do is turn on the television.

When the final day arrived, I was still dizzy and my equilibrium was off, which is why I was afraid to drive a car. As she had done every weekend during the month I was in rehab, Ta-rel drove the five hours from Gainesville to the facility near Ft. Lauderdale, then turned around and drove five hours back. This time I was going with her, and I was afraid. I got into the car and we drove awhile before stopping at a Cracker Barrel off the highway.

It was frightening being back in the world with all

these people and all the temptations. Everything is a trigger for an addict. It's all around you when you come out into the light of day. My head was still clearing for a couple months after I got out. It was weird. I was seeing things in a way I hadn't seen them in a long time. It was like, "Wow, look at that pretty pink cloud. Look at the butterfly. This is beautiful."

I was doing fine until we started to get closer to home. The closer we got, the more anxious I became. I suppose it was kind of like returning to the scene of the crime. Ta-rel had cleaned every corner of my very little house so I wasn't worried about a stray bottle of pills lying around. Still, as soon as I got home, I looked for an AA meeting to attend. I went to a meeting that first night and I didn't stop going to meetings for the next 364 days. They talked to us about the concept of "ninety in ninety," which refers to attending ninety meetings in the first ninety days after leaving rehab. I went an entire year without missing a single day and I needed every one of those meetings. Some people can return home and stay the course without going to meetings. Other people can't last more than a day or two without attending a meeting. It depends on the person and his or her support system. I needed somebody to talk to outside of my support group, which was essentially Ta-rel. She doesn't drink. She doesn't do drugs or anything like that. She had been with me through the worst of times over a five-year period. She saw my descent and I know she was worried about me slipping up. But she has been critical to my recovery.

It's probably reasonable to ask why she didn't do something as I was going deeper and deeper into my addictions, but the truth is there wasn't much she could have done. I had to hit bottom and make the decision on my own. I know this: She did what no one else would have done and that's take care of me. Most people would have left, and I wouldn't have blamed them. She stuck by me every step of the way, and a lot of those steps weren't pleasant. Ta-rel knew that if she didn't go to the liquor store and pick up a half gallon of vodka, then I would jump in my truck and do it myself. I'm sure she weighed the alternatives. I was going to get my stuff one way or another. At the end, I was going through a half gallon of vodka in less than two days. I had no business getting into a truck and starting the engine, much less driving anywhere.

The primary lesson of rehab is that recovery comes before everything and everyone. The counselors make sure you understand that nothing, especially work, is more important than an addict's recovery. Things were tight for us, but Ta-rel never said a word about me not working those first five or six months. I went to my meetings every night. I did what I was supposed to do every day. It might have looked like I was a lazy bastard taking advantage of this wonderful woman, but my job was to work on my sobriety and that's what I did. That's what I had to do. It took a long time to mess myself up to the point that I needed to get clean, and it was going to take a long time to crawl out of the hole I had dug for myself.

Eventually, I got a job through a connection I made at an AA meeting. For the first time in my adult life I had to go to work just like everyone else. To that point, I never had a job that required me to show up every day at the same place at the same time doing the same thing. A couple weeks after I left high school I started wrestling. What did I know about a real job? I worked as a security guard at a jewelry store, but it just wasn't me. I couldn't take the routine. I know that's how work is for most people. It's day after day after day. As hard as professional wrestling is, and it is extremely difficult physically, I love its free-form nature. I like the idea of being in a different place every night coming up with a new twist or turn in a program. I like interacting with different groups of fans and working in different venues. There's an electricity to it all. Needless to say, that charge was missing at the jewelry store.

Still, I didn't think about returning to wrestling for the first five or six months. I knew the possibility was out there, but I was focused on taking care of myself. I was so focused on my sobriety that I didn't let myself look too far into the future. When I did talk about it with my dad, he told me to forget about wrestling. He said I was too old, that wrestling was in my past. It was the same talk, and probably for many of the same reasons, I had heard from my father when I was young. He knew the business and he thought I'd be better off leaving it all behind and finding something else to do.

"Focus on your program, Dustin," he said. "You're too old to be wrestling anymore."

My dad had been around long enough to see, firsthand, how addiction messed up lives. With that said, he was an awesome father to me throughout all of this. The result is that we have developed the kind of father-son relationship that I craved when I was a little kid. We do just about everything together. We go turkey hunting, play golf, or just ride horses. We can have a good time together. After all these years and all the shared experiences, good and bad, there is only love between us now. I can't say enough about my dad. He's exactly the father I always wanted him to be and our relationship is truly wonderful. And the same goes for my stepmother, Michele. I love her to death.

I've said this before, but even at sixty-seven years of age and after nearly fifty years in the business he's as charismatic as ever. People have always loved Dusty Rhodes. It's incredible to me. I remember tagging with him back in the 1990s at a time when I had become popular. It didn't matter what I did. I might have had the fans behind me at the outset, but as soon as my dad slapped hands and entered the ring, that audience was all his. No matter what I did, the fans popped for my father. It was so cool.

He's always been my hero, but now that feeling comes from a much deeper place. I just hope he gets treated like the legend he is for all that he's accomplished. He should be remembered for being one of the original architects of professional wrestling. To this day, he remains one of the most charismatic guys ever to step inside a ring.

My counselor at the rehab facility wanted me to come back down to get my one-year medallion, but I just couldn't face that place again. I celebrated my first year drug and alcohol free with my sponsor. I celebrated my second year clean at home with Ta-rel. It's been two years and counting now, and I can't imagine ever going back to my former life. Aside from the obvious reasons, I feel like I owe something to Vince, Ann, and the company for taking a chance—chances—on me.

I had known Ann for a long time before I called and asked for help. She has always been so good to me in every way. She calls me her little miracle because there are other guys who haven't been able to conquer their demons even after coming out of rehab. I called Ann every week for a year after I got out. Sometimes I'd call her a couple times a week. She never failed to take the call, and she never failed to make every effort to have a meaningful conversation with me. It wasn't about her job. She just cared. That's not something you can fake. She's my third angel along with Dakota and Ta-rel. Ann's number is one I keep close to me at all times. I love her. I really do.

By the end of 2008, though, it was time to start living again.

TWELVE

THE RETURN

I always need to be doing something. That's a characteristic of attention deficit disorder. You have to remember that in those first few months out of rehab I had nothing but time on my hands. I didn't have much money and I didn't have a schedule full of commitments. I didn't have a job. All I had was time.

One day I decided to find a gym and start working out. Needless to say, I hadn't been very focused on my physical health and well-being for a long time. But I needed something to do, and going to the gym started to fill a little bit of that void. I didn't have the cash to hire a trainer, so I started slowly on my own. I was building up to what I called the three hundred, a combination of exercises that add up to three hundred repetitions. It's actually a form of circuit training that provides a total body workout. It's worked really well for me. I very quickly became hooked

on working out, and for the first time in my life I was going to the gym and working hard every day. At my heaviest, I weighed about three hundred pounds, which is a lot for me. Hell, it was all I could do to get through a match at the end. I'm lucky I didn't have a heart attack.

The workout routine was part of the program I selected for myself in recovery. It's become an important part of my life and since I've returned to wrestling. Not only can I keep up with all the young guys, but I've lost fifty-six pounds while adding a lot of muscle.

I don't know whether someone at the company heard about me working out, or it was just perfect timing, but one day the phone rang. It was John Laurinaitis. He wanted me to do a bit with Roddy Piper and the Honky Tonk Man at a Pay-Per-View in Phoenix at the end of 2008. I was going on seven months clean. I was getting stronger and working out harder. I just didn't know if I was strong enough. I was excited, but I was nervous, too.

By the time Laurinaitis called, I was feeling pretty good. But the idea of seeing everyone again made me very anxious. It was like leaving rehab. There is a part of you that fears leaving the facility because all the temptations and triggers are on the other side of those doors. That paranoia I had when I was all pilled up was still there, and it started to creep out as I got closer to the event. I knew I was doing good things. I knew my life was better than it had been in a very long time, but I still didn't know for sure whether I had what it took. Could I stay clean in that environment? It was a test. At the same time, I didn't have any questions or doubts about my ability to do the job. I have always known how to work. What I didn't know was whether I could keep up with the younger guys and go back to the rigorous daily routine. Specifically, I didn't know if I could do all that and stay the course on my recovery.

But everything went well in Phoenix. I did the Pay-Per-View, then television the next night and headed back home. I felt good about my performances, but I had no idea where they would lead. A couple months later, Laurinaitis called again. This time, he offered me a contract. The deal was designed so they could slowly work me back. It worked out exactly as they planned.

The next major test came months later when the company decided to send me to Europe. Once again, I was extremely nervous. That trip turned out to be the most intense test of my recovery. I was stuck in the bus with guys for four hours at a time, sometimes longer. I'd play cards, but there was alcohol on the bus. It wasn't like anybody was trying to get me to have a beer or anything like that. Everyone knew my situation and they were respectful, but it wasn't easy returning to that environment.

I had to stay completely focused all the time. That meant thinking about what I was doing just about every minute of every day. That kind of attention can be exhausting, but I never wavered.

About one year into my return, Vince came over one night. I can't count how many chances Vince had given me at that point, but it meant a lot that he wanted to talk to me. He didn't send somebody else with a message. He delivered it himself.

"Dustin, I want to start getting Goldust over again, but we have to take it easy."

I knew exactly what he was talking about. He was reminding me of the fact we had a PG audience on television, and I couldn't do the kind of the sick stuff I did back in the day. He wanted to make sure I understood the rules of the game—*all* the rules, including those that related to my continued employment. I couldn't go out there and go into business for myself doing nasty, dirty things on television. He was giving me another chance, another opportunity. And it felt good hearing that from Vince.

I also understood the part of that conversation that didn't involve Goldust. It didn't even require words. No one had to tell me that one of my responsibilities was to help some of the young guys. It might not sound like a big deal, but a lot of guys never understand the big picture.

They never figure out that wrestling is going to be around a long time after they are no longer able to climb into the ring. As a result, a lot of guys wind up on the outside looking in at exactly the time they could use the work. They get caught in things that don't matter. What they are really missing is an appreciation for the little things that make this business so great. They start losing matches that in the past they would have won. It's not losing that's an issue—it's how you lose that matters. There is a way to lose and still bring down the house. It's an art form, and some guys never learn to honor the subtleties of it.

I listened to Vince. When he finished, I said, "Thank you very much, sir. I won't be doing any of that stuff from the past. Thank you for the opportunity."

For the first few months I just followed the script. Whatever the writers gave me, I executed. It took some time before my creative juices started to flow again and I could provide the writers with ideas. That's what you have to be willing and able to do these days. It's not enough to show up for the match and perform. You have to be figuring out ways you can contribute. It's paid off for me to a degree I couldn't have imagined a couple years ago. I'm clicking on all cylinders now. I'm at the top of my game and I'm having fun.

I'm enjoying helping some of the young guys. I have

always been able to recognize potential. Whether it is a short conversation with a guy, or watching him work for a minute in the ring, I can tell. Some guys have it. Some guys don't. Let me lock up with a kid in the ring one time and I can tell you whether or not he has what it takes. I'm not the only one helping out the kids, though. Everyone is pretty much on the same page. We're all on the same team. Everyone seems willing to help, and that's a lot different compared to the past.

Every one of those matches hurt. I'd come home beat up and Ta-rel would be furious at Sheamus. I had the same experience with Ezekiel Jackson, the last guy I worked with at that time. I was like, "Man, take it easy. I don't know whether or not you are clear on this, but you don't actually have to hurt me. All you have to do is make it *look like* you're hurting me. That's actually fine." But it wasn't their fault. These guys are young and hungry. They want to learn and I was there to teach them the ins and outs. They were stiff, that's all. I was there to help smooth them out, which can be a physically demanding process.

Sheamus took it to the next level when he was with me. He has it and I'm not the only one who noticed. He was given an opportunity and he grabbed hold and didn't let go. People always ask what separates the guys who get to the top from the guys who don't get anywhere. It's not necessarily a lack of physical ability. The character issues are more important than pure athletic skill. It's heart, soul, and attitude. It takes all three. The guy has to be willing to work. He has to be willing to take direction. And he has to be willing to do what's necessary once he gets inside the ring. Everything has to become second nature and very, very smooth. It has to look like a ballet. That's how I learned to work, smooth and consistent. I've always been smooth in the ring because I had guys like Arn Anderson, Barry Windham, and others who taught me. I learned from true professional.

Arn, Ricky Steamboat, Bobby Eaton, Larry, and Barry—those guys did everything for me. Not only did they tell me what to do, but they told me how to do it and why it was necessary. I shut up and listened because I knew two things. First, they were great at what they did. They approached it like artisans approach their craft. They never took a night off, never mailed it in to collect a paycheck. Even when they were hurting, or were tired from an all-night car ride from the previous match, they always found a way to put on a great show. Second, they had my best interests at heart. I knew that because of how patient they were and how much time they took teaching me. They understood the importance of showing a young guy how to perform. They made me.

That's why I try to do as much as I can with the young

guys. I try to give to them what those veterans gave me early in my career.

In the end, Vince gave me another chance. I'm grateful for that opportunity. I'll pass on every bit of knowledge I have to the next generation of guys. It's the right thing to do. If I can do anything to help these guys get to the next level, then I'm happy to do so. I was one of those guys once.

THIRTEEN

THE BACKSIDE

These days no one ever talks about whether wrestling is real or fake. They'll say it's all scripted, and that's true up to a point. But the physical abuse wrestlers take in and out of the ring is real.

A fan can be sitting in the front row a few feet away from the ring. Being slammed onto the floor might not look that bad even up close, but that's only because we make it look easy. When we do that same move twenty or thirty times a match night after night, it's a whole other deal. Our bodies do get used to the physical toll. We know how to land and we know how to protect ourselves. Still, there are those moments when landing the wrong way can mess up your entire world. We might jump up like nothing just happened, but the pain is real.

The average person can't fall onto his back and pop right back up the way we do. One time? Maybe. Do that

over and over again one night, then get into a car and drive six hours to another town and do it again. It takes a toll. When fans ask me what it feels like to fall onto the mat, I tell them to fall straight back onto the grass. That's about what it feels like. The impact is enough to knock the wind out of the average person. Then, if you don't land right you can mess up your back pretty good. Our rings have four steel poles. The outer framing is all steel. There are steel crossbeams on the floor with two-by-six wood slats all the way across. There is quarter-inch plywood on top of that. Then there is a thin canvas that is pulled down and strapped tight. Basically, that's the ring. The give is not as much as you'd think, especially when you take a bump toward the outside edges. If I get slammed by Ezekiel or Vladimir Kozlov, I have lightning bolts shooting down my body. It's a big joke once we get behind the curtain, but sometimes my fingers go numb when I hit the floor.

Some of these young guys come in going one hundred miles an hour because they think it's going to be so easy. They're big and strong. They're in good shape. But if they do get pushed, you can see them start to slow down because they begin to realize that speed isn't the point. A great show is about what we give to the people. It's about entertaining each and every person in the audience. If I punch a guy in a real fight, then he's going to be hurt. If

I'm being punched in the ring, then the reaction on my face better sell that pain. That's why I love to watch Randy Orton. His theatrics—all the movements and facials—are probably the best around right now. A lot of guys can learn from watching Randy work.

Even hitting the ropes requires knowledge and finesse. Anybody who gets into the ring has to learn how to hit the ropes. You have to know how to plant your foot to give a move or take a move so that you don't blow out your knee. You have to know how to land on the mat with the theatrics of a stunt man. Big guys don't come off the top very often, but to this day I am amazed when I see it. Kane comes off the top rope with clotheslines and even I think, "How the hell does he do that without hurting himself?" Of course, the answer is that sometimes he does hurt himself. Kane knows how to roll, how to come off with that flying cow and still bounce back up. When he executes that move it's like I see it in slow motion, which is why I call it a flying cow. But don't think it doesn't hurt.

In 1998 I broke all the metacarpal bones across the top of my left hand giving Road Dog a bulldog near the end of the match in Utica, New York. It's a move I've done a million times, but on that night I landed with my hand backward. All it takes is a wrong move, or missing a fall by a couple inches. I had gloves on and I could feel my hand start to blow up inside the glove. I still had a few shots to give him, and he still had a few for me. I grabbed my hand after every one of them. Everything he gave me hurt my hand. It didn't matter where he hit me—the pain came straight out of my hand.

All of us deal with day-to-day pain of one degree or another. It's not necessarily any one shot, though it's certainly possible to tear up a knee or shred a muscle on any given night. Rather it's the day-to-day beating your body takes in the ring. Then there's the travel, which can be exhausting and most of the time is far from luxurious or exciting. It's hard for the average fan to appreciate the grueling preparation and logistics that go into a typical three- or four-day stretch on the road.

Here's a typical trip out west, one that I actually did in early 2010. I woke up Friday morning at four thirty, threw on my clothes, and drove fifteen to twenty minutes to the Gainesville airport. I always get to the airport early. There is no room for people who can't be counted on to arrive when they are supposed to. I don't check any bags unless I'm going on a long loop of at least a week or more. I checked in, got through security, and the plane took off at six fifty-five. By the time I got on the plane, I had been up for about two and half hours. Flying anywhere from Gainesville means a connection either through Atlanta or Charlotte, depending on the airline. I usually fly Delta, which takes me through Atlanta, which by itself can make for a long day. Sometimes I have to walk or run nearly a mile to reach my connection.

Then it was five hours on the plane to San Francisco. I didn't have enough mileage for an upgrade to first class, so I dragged my six-foot-four, 235-pound body back into coach. I arrived in San Francisco about one p.m. local time. On this trip, I was traveling with Kane. His flight was an hour late, so I spent that time hanging around the airport. Once he arrived, we went down to the rental car counter, arranged for a car, then drove 150 miles to the show. All the travel left no time to work out, so we drove directly to the arena. If it's a seven thirty show, we have to be in the arena no later than six thirty. I have to get dressed and paint up, which takes fifteen to twenty minutes. There isn't a makeup artist waiting for me. I have painted my own face from day one. I work on different designs all the time, so it takes time to get it just right.

By the time the show started, I'd been in three airports, driven 150 miles, and been awake for eighteen hours. Then I went to work. A show lasts two to three hours, depending upon the venue. When it was over, Kane and I packed up and headed back to the rental car. We had another 280-mile drive to the next city because we had a Saturday afternoon show. For the most part we are responsible for our expenses, which means we don't rent the best car and we certainly don't stay in the nicest hotel. I try to stay in Red Roof Inns or a La Quinta because they are cheap and the quality is pretty consistent. We pay for everything outside of airfare. Food, gas, hotel rooms, rental cars—it all comes out of our pockets.

By the time I got into bed that first night in California, I had been traveling and working for more than twenty-five hours. We checked in around three a.m., which was six a.m. East Coast time. I slept until around nine, then got up and found a gym so I could train before that day's show. Then it was a quick bite to eat and off to the arena for a three p.m. show. Around five or six we were back in the rental car for another 250-mile drive to the next city for a Sunday afternoon show.

For the first time since Thursday night, I got a pretty good night's sleep. The drive was only four or five hours, so we were in the hotel by ten. Sunday's schedule was the same as Saturday's, so it was up at nine, find a gym, grab some food, and head to the arena. The schedule was the same once the show ended, too, only this time we had a 450-mile drive. Since we were off on Monday, we split the trip in half. We drove for roughly four hours, found a hotel, and got a pretty good night's sleep. We finished off the second half of the drive on Monday, which is the first time since the trip started that we had time to relax a little bit. We still had four hours in the car, but we were in our hotel by the middle of the afternoon. We had time to get a nice meal. We didn't have to rush through a workout.

Tuesday was a television show, so the call time was early. We had to be at the arena by noon. The show didn't start for seven hours, but our day was filled up with pretaping for the show, photo shoots for the magazine, interviews, rehearsal, and all kinds of stuff. By the time the show ended, we'd been in the arena for at least ten hours. In California, particularly if we are near Los Angeles or San Francisco, there's still a chance to make the red-eye back east. It's a good news–bad news situation, though. If we do make the red-eye, then it's a race to the airport. I still have to connect through Atlanta, then drive home once I get to Gainesville. Just like the front end of the trip, the back end can result in at least a twenty-hour day. If I don't make the red-eye, then one of my two days off is spent traveling. The Delta flight to Gainesville leaves at six twenty a.m. and doesn't put me into Gainesville until after four p.m. To catch that flight I have to find a hotel Tuesday night. Depending on where we are, I probably don't get into bed until at least midnight. Then I'm back up at four a.m. so I can get to the airport with enough time to drop off the rental car, get through security, and make the flight.

By the time the four-day swing is over, I've been in at least four different airports, flown for twelve hours or more, and driven close to one thousand miles. I crash at home Wednesday night, spend Thursday trying to recover and pack up so I can do it all over again at the break of dawn on Friday or Saturday. And that's a pretty easy schedule. I've had days where there are three hundred miles between shows, followed by a 450-mile ride to the next one. I'll do that 280 to 300 days a year at this point in my career. There were some years when I was younger that I spent far more than three hundred days on the road.

Vince gives everybody the opportunity to work more and as a result make more money. It's up to us. If you don't take advantage of the opportunities that are presented to you, then you run the risk of getting stuck in one place and not advancing as fast or as far as you might like. It's all about personal responsibility. If you want the action, you have the chance to find it. But you have to make that move. No one else can do it for you. Back when I was younger, I complained about everything and I was making good money. It's no wonder they fired me for the stupid stuff I pulled. I wasn't being a reliable employee. In those days, I didn't recognize that I had the world in my hands. More than once, Vince gave me a great opportunity and I wasn't seeing clearly enough to recognize it. Now I do. I step up to the plate in every way I can. The result? A lot is happening and it's all good. I am getting my body into great shape. I'm doing really good work on television and everyone is taking notice. Vince knows. I come up with ideas. I give ideas. I'm patient in a way I never was when I was younger. I'm a living example that if you do those things, then good things will happen. And good things are happening to me. I'm happy with my job. I love this form of entertainment and it shows in my work.

I'll be honest, my body hurts. My lower back, left shoulder, and knees are sore all the time. It might look like we're walking just fine, but most people have no idea of the actual pain most guys live with. I'm living off Advil, which is a huge change for me compared to what I had been doing. But I'm living and working clean. Yes, I'm injured in more ways than anyone realizes, but I can't lie around and whine about it. I have to keep moving. I have to keep going to the gym every day because the work I do there keeps my joints loose and helps me avoid injury. Kane and I might get out of the car like a couple of grumpy old men, like Walter Matthau and Jack Lemmon. But we know how to turn it on when it's time to walk through that curtain. I get in that zone. I don't feel anything when it's time to perform.

Thankfully I never had any interest in steroids or anything like that. I always felt like I was big enough. The look that's in now is healthy and fit. Guys aren't jacked up and bulky anymore. Now they're in good, solid physical condition.

I'm not taking anything away from the old-school wrestlers who came up with my father, but those guys took a different kind of abuse than we do today. Everything is so fast paced and the falls are more dangerous today. Even after nearly fifty years in the ring, my dad doesn't have the kind of back problems Cody and I do. Those guys understood how to take a crowd and hold on to it sometimes for an hour. They were truly performing artists. These days you have to be a bionic man. Keep in mind, back then not all of those worked out. There were a few who trained and took it seriously, but most of the old-school wrestlers weren't going into the gym every day. Dad didn't work out. He knew how to work and he had charisma. It wasn't like he went to the gym and did body building every day. He was one of the few who had that giant body.

Today everybody is in shape. If you need to lose a few pounds, no one is afraid to tell you. You either do it or you're gone. We're all on television every week. You have to look good, but the way we wrestle today is so physically demanding that you can't afford not to be in shape. It's go, go, go all the time. It's still great, though, and that's what matters.

FOURTEEN

THE NEXT GENERATION

All in the family: My brother, Cody Rhodes.

I don't remember a whole lot about the day my brother, Cody, was born. I was seventeen years old and doing all the things a kid that age does—mostly chasing girls and playing sports. In other words, I wasn't changing diapers and babysitting a newborn even if he was my little brother. It's one of those things in life where your memory of it all comes in flashes of individual moments. I wasn't around much during Cody's younger years. I was out on the road trying to find my place in the family business and to one degree or another following our father around.

As Cody grew older, though, I remember him being adamant about staying away from wrestling. He wanted no part of it. He enjoyed seeing his brother perform and I know he was proud of what our dad accomplished, but Cody had seen the whole show from a different vantage point. When I was growing up, all I wanted to do was be near my dad. I wanted nothing more than to be a part of his life. If it meant leaving my mother and sister, moving across the country in the middle of high school, no problem. All I saw was the glamour of it all, bigger-than-life wrestlers like my dad and those hot bright lights shining down on the ring while fans screamed and cheered. I knew it was tough on my dad. Hell, it had been tough on me with him traveling all the time. Still, I never wanted to do anything else.

Cody was just the opposite. From a relatively young age, Cody's eyes were pointed toward Hollywood. He loved everything about the movie business. Becoming an actor was Cody's focus. He had other interests—ironically, wrestling was one of them—but Cody had a plan.

In some ways, Cody saw the dark side of it all. He moved around a fair amount growing up. He was born in North Carolina, moved to Texas as a little boy, and finished high school in Georgia. There were times when our dad was making a lot of money and everything was great. But there also were times when the family was closing in on bankruptcy. Pops has been extremely successful in the wrestling business, but it is a business. There are ups and downs, particularly when you are involved in the operations. Cody lived through a lot more of that as a kid than I ever did. Not only did he see the physical toll it took on our father, but he saw the stress that came with the financial side of things, too. And remember, Cody was old enough to understand what was going on when my dad and I went five years without speaking to each other. He saw what it did to the family. As I said, all I saw were the shining stars. Cody saw the same show, only with the curtains pulled back.

In high school, Cody was a dedicated one-sport athlete, and he was damn good. Cody was two-time state wrestling champion in Georgia. He wrestled at 189 pounds, which was a weight class dominated by the biggest, strongest, and best-conditioned kids. Cody lost only two matches his last two years. He was focused, talented, and competitive. As a big brother, it was really cool to see the person he was developing into.

It came together for all of us at the state championships Cody's senior year. The finals were held at the Macon Coliseum. Over the years, my dad and I had had some of our most memorable matches in that building. Of all the venues the Rhodeses have wrestled in, the Macon Coliseum was special. Right after I left Florida in the early 1990s for Total Nonstop Action, my dad and I had a really cool interview there. The story line was built around me looking for a tag-team partner. I had been wrestling with Barry Windham, but he got injured. Then I paired up with Arn Anderson, who turned on me and broke my arm. So that night I was looking for a new partner yet again. My dad took the microphone and the place went crazy. All he had to do was raise his arm and everyone would calm down. It was like a god had descended upon the building and he was going to announce the salvation plan for everyone in attendance.

Cody and me with our sisters Kristin (left) and Teil (right).

Pops said, "Stop looking for a partner, son. You can team up with me." The place went nuts. He held that entire building in the palm of his hand as he talked. One minute they were screaming at the top of their lungs, then next minute he'd raise that arm and you could hear a pin drop. To this day, people come up to me and say, "Man, I remember you and your dad in Macon."

Now it was Cody's turn in the same building, and the

place had the same kind of buzz. It was sold out. All the finalists walked down toward the floor from the top of the building. Music was blaring as these kids came down the steps. My dad, Diamond Dallas Page, and I were sitting right up against the mats. When they announced Cody's name I was like, "Wow. This kid is getting a pretty good pop." Parents sat on the opposite side of the mat from the coaches. We had the best seats in the house for Cody's title match. It was awesome, and so was Cody.

When he won, the whole building erupted. Dad and I shot out of our chairs and were going crazy. In that moment I reflected on the symmetry of it all. The three Rhodes boys all got a tremendous pop in the same building twenty years apart. It was unbelievable.

Cody had a lot of college wrestling offers from big schools, but the success never went to his head. I knew he respected what Dad and I did, but Cody was headed west. He packed his bags, found an agent, and moved to Los Angeles to become an actor. The determination and confidence that made him so good on the wrestling mat fueled his move. That's what he wanted to do and that's what he did. But acting is a tough business. Cody wasn't the only kid in the country heading out in search of his dreams. He landed some commercials and other work like that, but it didn't come together fast enough for him to survive out there.

By the time Cody returned to Georgia, Dad had started Turnbuckle Championship Wrestling and we were running a wrestling school, too. One day Cody came by the school. I was standing in the ring teaching. The students were spread out around the ring watching. I saw Cody and asked him to jump into the ring so that I could demonstrate a few things for the students.

Cody threw a smooth arm drag even though he had never really been in a ring before. I started out slow, then we started wrestling a little bit. I think I hurt him physically and I know I hurt his feelings. I was telling him how he had to pay his dues. I was being pretty rough with him and I actually made him cry. I hated myself for that. I was being very aggressive and rough, just trying to show him what this really feels like. But I took it too far and I felt awful.

But the rest is history. We can laugh about it now, but I still don't feel good about hurting him. He's my little brother. I had no business throwing him around like that. These days we'll fool around on the road when we're at the same television taping. We'll grab one another in fun and I'll remind him to take it easy on his big brother.

The one thing I knew from that first interaction with Cody in the ring is that he was a natural. All it took was one move and I knew Cody had more potential than all the rest of them combined. The kid had never done a single session in the ring and he was just so smooth. It was incredible.

Eventually Cody went off to Ohio Valley Wrestling, which was Vince's training facility in Louisville. I'll say this about Cody, he saw an opening and he grabbed hold and never let go. He paid his dues wrestling in front of small crowds like I did back in Florida. He made a little more than I did at his age, but that's a function of how far things have progressed. It's become a lot more sophisticated, and one company dominates the entire business now. I have no problem with the younger guys making as much money as they possibly can. If Cody can make twenty million times more than I ever make, great. I hope he does. I'll just ask him for a weekly allowance.

Aside from his physical skills, Cody has two very important things going for him. First, he's a smart kid. He knew what to do and how to conduct himself when an opportunity presented itself. Second, he's witty and he can talk. There are a lot of guys with athletic skill, but you can't teach intelligence. It's even harder to teach someone how to talk if he doesn't have the personality to make it all work. Cody is the whole package. He's got the world by the tail right now. All he has to do is keep a level head. There's no limit to what he can accomplish.

It's not easy, though. When you're young and rising like he is, it's easy to become frustrated because things aren't happening as fast as you want them to. About the only thing I have to tell Cody is, "Just be patient. You are doing

great. Vince loves you like a son. Just keep up the good work and everything is going to be great."

Over the next five years, Cody can become a power-house. We watch one another's work. He'll ask for advice, and I'm happy to help him any way I can. The kid has everything—personality, heart, soul, intelligence, attitude, and drive. Experience can't be taught, though. What you do in the ring has to make sense. You have to learn how to convey emotion. It's about the facials, the wrestler's reac-tions. Everything has to be so real that nobody questions it. Fans have to be able to see the pain. If you are confused, they have to see that, too. It's incredible when you actually pull it off. Cody understands that part of it. Cody is one of the young guys I would pay to watch right now and not just because he's my brother.

There are others, too. I would still pay to watch guys from my generation: Undertaker, Triple H. I love to watch Randy Orton. I'm really into Sheamus. I love what he's doing. Rey Mysterio? When you think he's dead after a flying fifteen-foot flip, Rey gets right up and kicks you in the head. He's like a baby bird falling out of a tree that just gets right back up and starts flying. He's unbelievable to watch. I have never seen him have a bad match. Even when he's having a match with somebody who might not be having a good night, Rey can pull a damn good match. He's probably my favorite guy to watch.

Shawn Michaels is the very best worker there is. It doesn't matter whether you watch what he was doing at the beginning of his career or right now. He's one of the best. One of the hardest-working guys in the company is Chris Jericho. Christian is fun to watch and I love his work ethic. Even when a great match isn't needed, he goes out there and gives you one anyway just because he loves what he does. Shawn is the same way. If you have two guys in the ring with the same mind-set, then you're going to have a hell of a match. No one can have a bad match if he is in there with Shawn Michaels or Chris Jericho.

CM Punk is a really good worker and he's fun to watch. The thing with Triple H is that he can flat out work. He has that old-school ethic and he's always completely tuned in to what he's doing. When there is a spot in a match or a show when something is really needed, Hunter comes through every time. If there is an extra five or ten minutes on television, it doesn't matter whether he learns about it before the match or at the last second. He gets everyone calm, then he comes up with something that's really good. He's one of those rare guys who are larger than life. Undertaker is the same way. His entrance has never changed, and I still think it's the best around. Orton is another guy who, when he turns it on, it's "Wow!"

That's where Cody is heading. He's the next link in the Rhodes family chain.

FIFTEEN

ANGELS ON THE
ROAD AHEAD

I don't think I have ever been better at my work than I am right now. I am a living example of the idea that good things come to those who listen, take suggestions, and work with passion and focus. I'm leaner, faster, and better at my job than I've ever been. I've worked hard to hone my craft, and it shows.

I didn't think I could go out there and wrestle without painkillers rolling through my body. I've got aches and pains, but I'm working clean and sober. It's the only way to go. Even though I've been doing Goldust since 1995, the crowds are getting louder for me. My entrance may not be as elaborate as Undertaker's, but mine is right behind his in terms of impact. Goldust is one of the last gimmicks, a character-driven personality, and they still pop loud when I walk out. After all that I've been through, it means a lot to be respected. It's unfortunate that I'm at the tail end of my career, but I'm all about keeping my performance at the top. Right now everyone tells me I look a lot younger than my age. I was looking at a picture of myself the other day when I was twenty-one or twenty-two years old, and I look just like that now. With the paint, I don't age. As long as I can keep my body in shape, I should be fine.

Left to right: Teil, Dad, my stepmom, Michele,
Dakota, Cody, and me.

Why do I know I'll never drink or do drugs again? I spent years abusing myself and I became something I never thought I'd become—undependable. I promised myself that I was going earn back the respect I had built up over nearly two decades. I have nothing to complain about these days because I am fortunate to be alive. I know that. Right now, I'm just paying my dues and working hard to improve every day. For the first time in a long time, I am seeing life through clear eyes. If I have a bad day, I know it will pass. A few years ago, every day was a bad day. Now I can have a bad day and still know I have a great life.

Just waking up in the morning and being able to make lunch for Dakota is a gift. I am gaining back her respect and trust by being a positive factor in her life. I can't tell you what a thrill it is to have her want to talk to me about her life. Dakota and I are closer now than we have ever been. I know I can't take back those five awful years when I was filling myself with alcohol and drugs, so I'm moving forward to make the best years of my life those in front me. Too many good things are happening to think any other way.

I know I'll have many more years fighting those demons trying to nip away at me. I'll keep them at bay. I am straight up about the fact I am going to take care of myself first and foremost. People respect that. My daughter understands where I'm coming from and she respects me for being honest about what I need to do for myself. Though I love what I do as much as I ever have, I hate being away from her. We are connected the way every father and daughter should hope to be connected. Just thinking about her brings tears to my eyes.

When Dakota was born she had some breathing problems. The doctors put her under a heat lamp and worked to help her breathe. In that same room there was another baby screaming uncontrollably. I asked a nurse what was wrong with the other baby. It turned out the mother had been a crack addict. She died during childbirth and the newborn was coming down off the crack in her system. Then I looked over at Dakota, and she wasn't crying at all. It was almost like she had a little smile on her face under those big bright eyes. I remember thinking how lucky I was, and how fortunate Dakota was to have two parents so devoted to her. She was holding my little finger, and to this day it amazes me the way she looked into my eyes.

With Kristin, one of my angels.

She's one of my angels who stood by my side in the darkest moments of my life. I haven't talked enough about my sister Kristin, but she never wavered in her love and support of me. We protected one another growing up in Austin when my dad left. Throughout my life whenever she felt like I had a problem, or I was struggling with something, she didn't hesitate to find a flight and come see me. She's a remarkable person with an amazing capacity for love.

Through it all, though, I'm still Dustin. As I've always said, I don't want to kill all my demons because then there won't be any angels.

Printed in the United States
By Bookmasters